The Family History And Genealogy of Johann Ferdinand Thöne and Maria Anna Juliana Antonette Drewes

Dr. Christoph Bartneck

Dr. Christoph Bartneck is a Senior Lecturer and Academic Director at the University of Canterbury, New Zealand. He and his family leave in Christchurch, after having spend time in Japan, Netherlands, Germany, Denmark and the USA.

© 2011 by Christoph Bartneck

Printed by CreateSpace, USA

ISBN-13:   978-1463607883

ISBN-10:   1463607881

Tree illustration by DragonArtz

Table of contents

Introduction

A large illustrated family tree had been hanging in my parent's living room for more than twenty years before I got interested in it. I was aware of your ancestors since my childhood, but it was probably the birth of my own children that sparked my desire to document our heritage. My children are growing up in the distant New Zealand, far away from both our families. I wanted to be able to explain to my children where their family is from.

Once I started investigating my parent's illustrated family tree, I noticed some striking inconsistencies. Some relationships in the tree were simply impossible, such as a daughter being born before her parents. My parents did not have computers at their disposal when piecing together all the information and hence these errors are easy to understand. Their work had been based on hand written copies of an illusive family tree at distant relatives. Already my grandparents had copied this tree in writing. It took my parents some time before they could locate the original tree at Heinrich Meiwes in Rietberg. They photographed the tree, added the more recent relatives, and ask a graphic designer to draw the tree. It took several months to complete the drawing. Finally my parents were able to hang the illustrated family tree in our living room. However, the exact source of the tree at Heinrich Meiwes was not documented in the illustrated tree.

My scientific training made me sensitive for the need of proper referencing sources. The illustrated tree was only an indication, but certainly not a proof of our heritage. I started to investigate the sources for all the information available and in my uncle Ulrich Hoppe, I found a companion who shared my interest in our family tree. He had already collected the old family books of our relatives and my first task was to catalog all the available information from these documents. I was also able to buy an old book about the Thöne family, which turned out to be the key to our lineage. [ref thoene buch]

Dr. Wilhelm Bernhard Valentin Thöne (born August 24th, 1893), a dentist living in Düsseldorf, wrote a detailed account of his family tree and published it in 1938. His genealogical interest went far beyond the required heritage proofs in Nazi Germany. The importance of this book for our family tree cannot be underestimated. It documents two lines into the past. One is the line of the family Thöne up to the year 1282, the other is a more general aristocratic line that goes back to Karl the Great and beyond. It separates from the Thöne line at the point of Johann Ferdinand Thöne's wife, Maria

Anna Juliana Antonette Drewes (born December 3, 1780, death December 17th, 1846). Her parents connect to the aristocracy through Franz Dietrich Von Bose (see Figure 1 and on page 68, person nr. 20) all the way back to Arnulf von Metz (born ca 584, died ca 641).

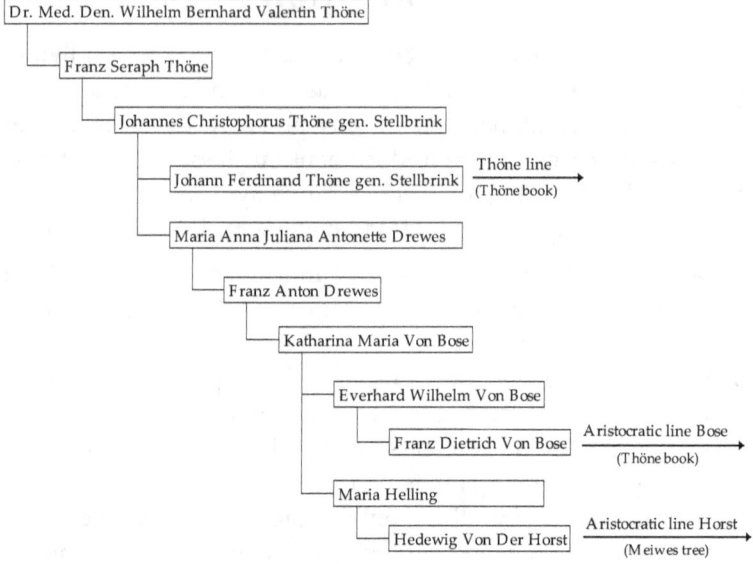

Figure 1: The split of the three ancestor lines.

When I visited Heinrich Meiwes myself in 2010 to investigate the source of the family tree that my parents had photographed, I discovered that Dr. Wilhelm Thöne was also the author of this family tree. This third line separates from the Bose line at Katharina Maria Von Bose (see Figure 1). Her mother, Maria Helling, connects to the aristocracy through Hedwig Von Der Horst (see page 68, person nr. 23). The Horst line goes back to Liudolf Liudolfinger (born ca 805, died March 12th, 866).

These two aristocratic lines reconnect through the marriage of Zwentibold (Karolinger) (born ca 870, death August 13th, 900) with Oda (Liudolfinger) in the year 897. Oda was the daughter of Otto I. Der Erlauchte (Liudolfinger, born before 866, death November 30th 912) to whom the Horst line connects. Zwentibold is a descendent of Ludwig I. der Fromme Karolinger (born 778, death June 20th, 840) with his first wife Irmingard (born 780, death 818). The Bose line goes back to Ludwig I. through Ludwig's children with his second wife Judith von Bayern (born 795, death 843).

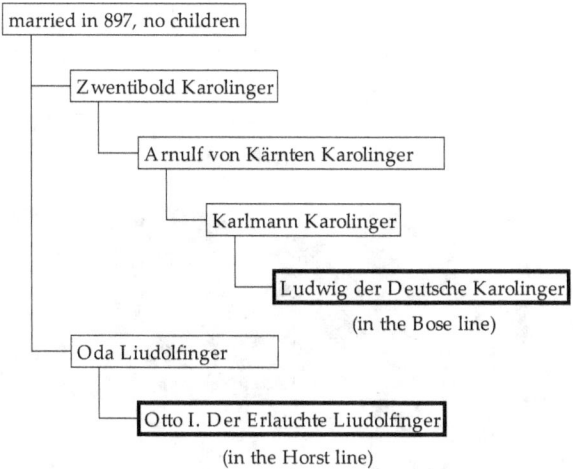

Figure 2: The connection between the Bose and Horst line.

As amazing as these three trees are, we still had no full proof on how our family connects to Wilhem Thönes family tree. The oldest document in our possession was the family book of Heinrich Klahold and Theresia Hartman, the parents of my grandmother. In the city archive of Paderborn I found the birth certificate of Theresia Hartman, that confirmed that she was the daughter of Johan Eduard Hartmann. In December 2010 I visited the Erzbischöfliches Generalvikariat in Paderborn together with Ulrich. There we could finally find the missing piece of the puzzle. In the church book we found the proof that Johann Eduard Hartman was the son of Franciscus Antonius (Anton) and Anna Maria Theresia Thöne (see Figure 3). This couple is listed in Wilhem Thönes book on page 151 in the section B) Linie Stellbrink. Anna Maria Theresia was the daughter of Johann Ferdinand Thöne, named "Stellbrink".

Figure 3: Birth entry of Johann Eduard Hartman in the church book of Wewer.

My contribution to Wilhelm Thöne's work is merely the documentation and correction of his work, and the extension into the younger generations. In particular the descendants of my grand-grand mother is well documented.

My grand mother had seven sisters and four brothers. These descendants still share are sense for a common root and many followed Ulrich's invitation to a family reunion in 2006. Figure 4 shows the relatives present on that day. In total Heinrich Klahold and Theresia Hartman have 71 descendants as of April 29th, 2011 and more will hopefully follow.

Figure 4: Living descendants of Heinrich Klahold and Theresia Hartman (2006)

The discovery of the Horst line also brought forward some unexpected connections. First, the point at which the two aristocratic lines separate is the wife of Everhard Wilhem Von Bose, Maria Helling, who was born in Vlotho. I grew up in Vlotho myself and I was surprised to discover relatives so close to home. Second, Maria Hellwigs grandfather in law Arnold Von Der Horst (Drosten of Vlohto, death 1641), is mention on the Wittekindstein, located on the side of the Wittekinstrasse. I spend my early childhood less than a kilometer away from the stone at the Bonnebergerstrasse. Klaus Bartneck took a photo of the inscription in 2010 (see Figure 5). Arnold Von Der Horst is believed to have donated a church window to the church in Valdorf, which depicted his family emblem. [ref history book]. However, they window may have been lost in 1836.

It also becomes apparent that the our family history is dominated by women. In comparison, little is know about my father's ancestors or the ancestors of my mother's father or even the ancestors of my grandmother's the father. The trail of my father's ancestors goes back to the city of Breslau in the former German state of Schlesien, which is today a part of Poland. Most records seem to have been lost during the second world war.

Figure 5: Inscription on the Wittekindstein

The war has certainly been a difficult time but our family lost Franz Klahold (born December 22nd, 1922, death March 2nd southwest of Varna, Estland). Franz joined the army on October 9th, 1941. He served in Braunschweig, Leningrad, Oranienbaum and Narwa. He was killed by a shrapnel to his head and he is buried in the graveyard of the 170. Infrantie-Division in Toila (Estland). All others survived, but I have not been able to find conclusive records for everyone.

Johann Heinrich Hoppe joined the NSDAP on September 1st, 1938 with the membership number 7016097. Heinrich joined the army on September 20th, 1940. He served as an ambulance driver from 1941-1944. He was located in Drontheim (Norway). In 1944 he was send to the east front.

Heinrich was captured by the Russian Army at the Sereth river, close to the Hungarian border, on September 6th, 1944. He appeared first in the Russian records as being placed in the hospital camp nr. 3006 in Drushkowka, Doneszk, Ukraine. From there, he was registered in the Russian camp (Gulag) nr, 217 and nr. 247 in the area of Doneszk, Ukraine. From his own recollection, he was imprisoned in Konstantinovka, Doneszk, Ukraine. He was released from his imprisonment in the camp Gronefelde (Frankfurt an der Oder) on August 16th, 1949 after five years in the Russian gulags.

Paul Wilhelm Bartneck served in the German Army in the 5. Kompanie Panzer-Regiment 11. He operated in the Netherlands, Belgium, Germany and White Russia. He was wounded on December 14th, 1942 with a shrapnel to his head. He was returned back to Paderborn and continued to serve in the army. In 1943 he was returned into the active troops (Panzer Abteilung 505). He then served in Russia, Ukraine, Normandie and Germany. He was registered by a British Release unit, but no details of any war imprisonment is available.

Eduard Hartman Eduard was a professional soldier even before the war. On January 1st 1936 he joined the Navy. He was first stationed at the III. Schiffsstammabteilung der Nordsee, Wesermünde. Next, he participated in the Spanish civil war on board the Kreuzer Köln (1937-1939). From December 17th, - August 18th 1943 he was stationed on the U-Boot "U 953". Since September 19th 1943 he was stationed at the 1. U-Ausbildungsabteilung, Plön. Next, he was registered from September 19th 1944 - December 18th 1944 at the 4. U-Flottille (ohne Bootsangabe). Since September 19th 1944 he was at the 6. Kriegsschiffbaulehrabteilung, Bremen; Baubelehrung für"U 3014". His last grade was "Obersteuermann". On August 12th, 1945 he was released from the British authorities with the registration U3014. He received the "Spanienkreuz in Bronze" on June 6th 1939 and the "Medaille zur Erinnerung an den 01 .10.1938" on December 20th 1939.

But I shall not forget my Japanese relatives. In February 2010 I stayed for several months at Tatsuya and Etsuoko Masuoka. During this time I tried to document this side of our family tree, which had its own difficulties. The language barrier could relatively easily be overcome, due to Tatsuya's excellent command of the English language. The problem was more in the fact that the Japanese temples and shrines did often not keep records of births, marriages and deaths. It was up to the families to document their heritage. But luckily we could find some old documents and with the help of Etsuko and Tatsuya, we were able to trace back this line for many generations. We were even able to discover some old photographs.

This book is structured in several sections. The first three sections will all have Johannes Ferdinand Thöne (called Stellbring) and his wife Maria Anna Juliana Antonette Drewes as their starting points. The first section shows all the descendants, the second the Thöne line and the third section the two aristocratic lines. Next I will show the ancestors of the family Bartneck and Masuoka.

I hope that you enjoy reading this book and that it gives you a good overview of our family and its heritage. There are more than 980 persons in my database and there is no single way to present the data. It will always have to be a subset in order to present the relationships between the people in an understandable structure. I still hope that this family tree is of use to you. Please send me all your comments, including extensions and corrections to christoph@bartneck.de.

The Descendants of Thöne & Drewes

First Generation
————————— ✣ —————————

1. Johann Ferdinand Thöne gen. Stellbrink [1]. Johann Ferdinand died in Paderborn-Wewer, Paderborn, on 21 Apr 1813; he was 47. Born on 20 Jan 1766 in Altenbeken, Paderborn. Occupation: Vollmeier.

On 26 Sep 1800 when Johann Ferdinand was 34, he first married **Maria Anna Juliana Antonette Drewes**, daughter of Franz Anton Drewes (28 Oct 1751-21 Nov 1789) & Anna Maria Elisabeth Claes (28 Oct 1751-2 Jun 1814). [2] Born on 3 Dec 1780 in Kempen, Viersen. Maria Anna Juliana Antonette died in Paderborn-Wewer, Paderborn, on 17 Dec 1846; she was 66.

They had the following children:

2	i.	Maria Elisabeth (9 Oct 1805-)
3	ii.	Anna Maria Theresia (22 Nov 1813-27 Dec 1867)
4	iii.	Bernhard Gen. Mühlenburs (2 Nov 1810-16 Apr 1885)
5	iv.	Anna Maria Theresia (21 Apr 1808-14 Apr 1841)
6	v.	Johannes Christophorus gen. Stellbrink (30 Mar 1803-5 Aug 1882)

maybe he did not die in 1813, because a child of his was born that year. Or maybe he died not in Wewer. The Wewever death registry did not have an entry for him.

In 1794 when Johann Ferdinand was 27, he second married **Elisabeth Block Gen. Stellbrink** [1]. Elisabeth died on 3 Jul 1800 in Paderborn-Wewer, Paderborn.

Erbtochter auf Stellbrinkshofe. She had two children with Johann, but both of them died at young age.

They had one child:

7	i.	Anna Maria (4 Sep 1800-)

Second Generation
———————— ⁘ ————————

2. Maria Elisabeth Thöne. Born on 9 Oct 1805.

On 14 May 1829 when Maria Elisabeth was 23, she married **Franz Josef Hartmann** in Paderborn-Wewer, Paderborn. [1] Occupation: Schreiner.

3. Anna Maria Theresia Thöne. Anna Maria Theresia died in Paderborn-Wewer, Paderborn, on 27 Dec 1867; she was 54. [1] Born on 22 Nov 1813 in Paderborn-Wewer, Paderborn.

Franciscus Antonius (Anton) Hartmann

On 27 Aug 1839 when Anna Maria Theresia was 25, she married **Franciscus Antonius (Anton) Hartmann**, son of Johannes Hartmann & Maria Theodora Westermeyer, in Paderborn-Wewer, Paderborn. Franciscus Antonius (Anton) died on 3 Jul 1887; he was 81. Born on 13 Mar 1806 in Paderborn-Wewer, Paderborn. Occupation: Schreiner.

They had the following children:

8	i.	Anna Theresia Wilhelmine (27 Nov 1857-)
9	ii.	Heinrich (28 Apr 1849-5 Aug 1908)
10	iii.	Johann Eduard (1 Jan 1846-1933)
11	iv.	Anna Bernardina (16 Feb 1841-26 Feb 1844)
12	v.	Bernard (25 Jul 1856-)
13	vi.	Maria Anna (22 May 1843-)

4. Bernhard Thöne Gen. Mühlenburs. Bernhard died on 16 Apr 1885; he was 74. Born on 2 Nov 1810.

On 29 Jul 1841 when Bernhard was 30, he married **Theresia Schäfers Gen. Mühlenburs**, daughter of Johann Schäfers (-1 May 1866). Theresia died on 1 May 1866.

Theresia married Bernhard after her first husband died.

They had the following children:

    14   i.   Maria Elisabeth Therese (1844-1848)
    15   ii.   Clemens August (1846-1853)

5. Anna Maria Theresia Thöne. Anna Maria Theresia died on 14 Apr 1841; she was 32. Born on 21 Apr 1808 in Paderborn-Wewer, Paderborn.

On 16 Apr 1832 when Anna Maria Theresia was 23, she married **Heinrich Jakobs gen. Brockmeyer**. Occupation: Vollmeier (Vollspänner).

Johannes Christophorus Thöne gen. Stellbrink

6. Johannes Christophorus Thöne gen. Stellbrink [1]. Johannes Christophorus died in Paderborn-Wewer, Paderborn, on 5 Aug 1882; he was 79. Born on 30 Mar 1803 in Paderborn-Wewer, Paderborn. Occupation: Landwirt und Gemeinderat.

On 23 Jun 1840 when Johannes Christophorus was 37, he married **Anna Maria Richter** [1], daughter of Joseph Conrad Richter (27 Mar 1799-1 Feb 1860) & Anna Katharina Hapig (27 Sep 1798-1 Apr 1875), in Paderborn-Wewer, Paderborn. Born on 7 May 1820 in Delbrück-Bentfeld, Paderborn. Anna Maria died in Paderborn-Wewer, Paderborn, on 8 Aug 1867; she was 47.

They had the following children:

    16   i.   Anna Bernhardine (1 Jun 1841-)

17	ii.	Konrad Joseph gen. Stellbrink (21 Aug 1842-5 Apr 1909)
18	iii.	Maria Elisabeth Therese (30 Sep 1844-4 Feb 1908)
19	iv.	Aloysia Maria (26 Jan 1848-1 Jun 1907)
20	v.	Johann Heinrich (13 Sep 1853-17 May 1926)
21	vi.	Kaspar (18 Jan 1856-)
22	vii.	Anna Elisabeth (11 Mar 1858-)
23	viii.	Bernhard gen. Steffensmeier (18 Nov 1846-12 Apr 1928)
24	ix.	Franz Seraph (4 Feb 1851-22 Jun 1906)

7. Anna Maria Thöne. Born on 4 Sep 1800 in Paderborn-Wewer, Paderborn. [2]

Third Generation

8. Anna Theresia Wilhelmine Hartmann. Born on 27 Nov 1857 in Paderborn-Wewer, Paderborn. [2]

9. Heinrich Hartmann. Born on 28 Apr 1849 in Paderborn-Wewer, Paderborn. [2] Heinrich died on 5 Aug 1908; he was 59. [2]

Johann Eduard Hartmann

10. Johann Eduard Hartmann. Johann Eduard died in 1933; he was 86. Born on 1 Jan 1846 in Paderborn-Wewer, Paderborn. [2] Occupation: Zimmermeister.

aufebahrt in scheune. ganz wewer war zur wewer beerdigt. st baptist friedhof.

Theresia Berhorst

On 26 Nov 1879 when Johann Eduard was 33, he married **Theresia Berhorst**, daughter of Johannes Berhorst (8 Apr 1816-) & Anna Theodora Büllmann (10 Nov 1822-), in Paderborn-Wewer, Paderborn. Born on 22 Jan 1854 in Paderborn-Wewer, Paderborn. [2] Theresia died in Paderborn-Wewer, Paderborn, on 16 May 1906; she was 52. [2], [3]

They had the following children:

25	i.	Anna
26	ii.	Theresia (3 Dec 1883-14 Mar 1965)
27	iii.	Lorenz
28	iv.	Franz
29	v.	Maria
30	vi.	Kristiane

11. Anna Bernardina Hartmann. Born on 16 Feb 1841 in Paderborn-Wewer, Paderborn. [2] Anna Bernardina died in Paderborn-Wewer, Paderborn, on 26 Feb 1844; she was 3. [2]

12. Bernard Hartmann. Born on 25 Jul 1856 in Paderborn-Wewer, Paderborn. [2]

13. Maria Anna Hartmann [2]. Born on 22 May 1843 in Paderborn-Wewer, Paderborn. [2]

14. Maria Elisabeth Therese Thöne. Born in 1844. Maria Elisabeth Therese died in 1848; she was 4.

15. Clemens August Thöne. Born in 1846. Clemens August died in 1853; he was 7.

Anna Bernhardine Thöne

16. Anna Bernhardine Thöne [1]. Born on 1 Jun 1841.

On 7 Oct 1862 when Anna Bernhardine was 21, she married **Konrad Agethen gen. Burschäfer** [1] in Lichtenau-Henglarn, Paderborn. Occupation: Vollmeier (Vollspänner).

Konrad Joseph Thöne gen. Stellbrink

17. Konrad Joseph Thöne gen. Stellbrink [1]. Born on 21 Aug 1842. Konrad Joseph died in Paderborn-Elsen, Paderborn, on 5 Apr 1909; he was 66. Occupation: Landwirt und Gemeindevorsteher in Wewer.

Maria Ludowika Meschede

On 17 Feb 1870 when Konrad Joseph was 27, he married **Maria Ludowika Meschede** [1], daughter of Joseph Meschede gen. Kamp & Ludowika

Kloppenburg gen. Göke. [1] Born in 1849 in Büren-Wewelsburg, Paderborn. Maria Ludowika died in Paderborn-Wewer, Paderborn, on 30 Apr 1886; she was 37.

They had the following children:

31	i.	Johann Jospeh (20 Dec 1870-30 Jun 1875)
32	ii.	Johann Joseph (12 Jul 1872-2 Sep 1902)
33	iii.	Bernhard (11 Mar 1874-1 Jan 1884)
34	iv.	Theresia (1 Oct 1878-22 Oct 1898)
35	v.	Johann Franz (9 Aug 1882-19 Jan 1884)
36	vi.	Franz (22 Mar 1886-14 Apr 1886)
37	vii.	Maria Ludowika gen. Luise (1 May 1876-1957)

18. Maria Elisabeth Therese Thöne [1]. Born on 30 Sep 1844. Maria Elisabeth Therese died in Delbrück-Südhagen, Paderborn, on 4 Feb 1908; she was 63.

On 17 Feb 1870 when Maria Elisabeth Therese was 25, she married **Heinrich Graute** [1]. Occupation: Gutsbesitzer, Gastwirt und Gemeindevorsteher.

19. Aloysia Maria Thöne [1]. Born on 26 Jan 1848. Aloysia Maria died on 1 Jun 1907; she was 59.

On 17 Feb 1870 when Aloysia Maria was 22, she married **Karl Meier gen. Pulsen** [1] in Paderborn-wewer, Paderborn.

20. Johann Heinrich Thöne [1]. Born on 13 Sep 1853. Johann Heinrich died in paderborn-wewer, Paderborn, on 17 May 1926; he was 72.

21. Kaspar Thöne [1]. Born on 18 Jan 1856. Kaspar died in Dortmund-Barop, Dortmund.

22. Anna Elisabeth Thöne [1]. Born on 11 Mar 1858.

Anna Elisabeth married **Heinrich Borgmeier** [1]. Born in Salzkotten, Paderborn. Occupation: Stellmachermeister.

Bernhard Thöne gen. Steffensmeier

23. Bernhard Thöne gen. Steffensmeier [1]. Born on 18 Nov 1846 in Paderborn-wewer, Paderborn. Bernhard died on 12 Apr 1928; he was 81. Occupation: Landwirt.

Ludowika Steffens

On 7 Jul 1874 when Bernhard was 27, he married **Ludowika Steffens**. Born on 31 Jan 1852. Ludowika died on 2 Nov 1928; she was 76.

She married Bernhard after her previous husband died.

Franz Seraph Thöne

24. Franz Seraph Thöne [1]. Born on 4 Feb 1851. Franz Seraph died in Düsseldorf on 22 Jun 1906; he was 55. Occupation: Kunstmaler.

Maria Dössing

On 5 Oct 1882 when Franz Seraph was 31, he married **Maria Dössing** [1], daughter of Johann Dössing & Franziska Jacobs, in Paderborn-Wewer, Paderborn. Born on 2 May 1851. Maria died in Düsseldorf on 12 Aug 1914; she was 63.

They had the following children:

38	i.	Dr. Med. Den. Wilhelm Bernhard Valentin (24 Aug 1893-1957)
39	ii.	Dr. Phil. Johannes Franz Seraph (19 Nov 1884-1945)
40	iii.	Dr. Jur. Joseph Anton (14 May 1887-7 Oct 1916)
41	iv.	Dr. Phil. Aloys Franz Anton (23 Sep 1888-1967)
42	v.	Maria Gertrud (21 May 1890-1966)
43	vi.	Antonia Elisabeth (28 May 1896-1952)
44	vii.	Anton Franz Xaver (14 May 1891-22 Jun 1958)

Fourth Generation

⁜

Anna Hartmann

25. Anna Hartmann.

Conrad Drewes

Anna married **Conrad Drewes**.

Theresia Hartmann

26. Theresia Hartmann. Born on 3 Dec 1883 in Paderborn-Wewer, Paderborn. [4], [5] Theresia died in Paderborn on 14 Mar 1965; she was 81. [4], [3]

Heinrich Klahold

On 14 Oct 1910 when Theresia was 26, she married **Heinrich Klahold**, son of Franz Klahold (19 Aug 1846-2 Jan 1918) & Maria Brockmann (10 Dec 1851-27 Mar 1918), in Paderborn-Wewer, Paderborn. [6], [3] Born on 13 Jul 1883 in Altenbeken, Paderborn. [7] Heinrich died in Paderborn on 7 Mar 1965; he was 81. [3] Occupation: Ober Lokführer. [8]

They had the following children:

45	i.	Maria (8 Aug 1911-10 Oct 1987)
46	ii.	Anna Theresia (18 Aug 1912-Apr 2010)
47	iii.	Elisabeth Maria (10 Nov 1913-24 Apr 1993)
48	iv.	Maria Wilhelmina (9 Feb 1915-23 Dec 2001)
49	v.	Gertrud Johanna (8 Mar 1916-19 May 1935)
50	vi.	Johanna Christine (25 May 1917-)
51	vii.	Theresia Henriette (28 Dec 1918-)
52	viii.	Eduard Johannes (9 May 1920-1 Jun 1920)
53	ix.	Josef Franz (14 May 1921-31 Mar 1937)
54	x.	Franz (22 Dec 1922-2 Mar 1944)
55	xi.	Heinrich Johannes (20 Feb 1924-10 Apr 2010)
56	xii.	Angela Genoveva (9 Apr 1926-)

Lorenz Hartmann

27. Lorenz Hartmann.

Maria Catharina Stegemann

Lorenz first married **Maria Catharina Stegemann**. Born in 1892. Maria Catharina died in 1931; she was 39.

They had the following children:

| 57 | i. | Eduard (23 Jul 1917-13 Jan 2001) |

58	ii.	Franz (7 Aug 1924-20 Jun 1998)
59	iii.	Johannes (24 Nov 1919-8 Aug 1998)
60	iv.	Elisabeth
61	v.	Gertrud

Lorenz second married **Elisabeth Rosendahl**. Born in 1890. Elisabeth died in 1961; she was 71.

Franz Hartmann

28. Franz Hartmann.

Theresia Hesse

Franz married **Theresia Hesse**, daughter of unknown Hesse.

Maria Hartmann

29. Maria Hartmann.

Kristiane Hartmann

30. Kristiane Hartmann.

Josef Hesse

Kristiane married **Josef Hesse**.

They had the following children:

62	i.	Eduard
63	ii.	Paula
64	iii.	Stefan
65	iv.	Theresia
66	v.	Maria

31. Johann Jospeh Thöne [1]. Born on 20 Dec 1870. Johann Jospeh died on 30 Jun 1875; he was 4.

32. Johann Joseph Thöne [1]. Born on 12 Jul 1872. Johann Joseph died on 2 Sep 1902; he was 30. Occupation: Landwirt.

33. Bernhard Thöne [1]. Born on 11 Mar 1874. Bernhard died on 1 Jan 1884; he was 9.

Theresia Thöne

34. Theresia Thöne [1]. Born on 1 Oct 1878. Theresia died on 22 Oct 1898; she was 20.

35. Johann Franz Thöne [1]. Born on 9 Aug 1882. Johann Franz died on 19 Jan 1884; he was 1.

36. Franz Thöne [1]. Born on 22 Mar 1886. Franz died on 14 Apr 1886; he was <1.

Maria Ludowika Thöne gen. Luise

37. Maria Ludowika Thöne gen. Luise [1]. Born on 1 May 1876. Maria Ludowika died in 1957; she was 80.

Heinrich George Meiwes

On 9 Sep 1903 when Maria Ludowika was 27, she married **Heinrich George Meiwes** [1] in Paderborn-Elsen, Paderborn. Born on 15 May 1886 in Delbrück-Westenholz, Paderborn. Heinrich George died in Dec 1962; he was 76.

They had the following children:

67	i.	Joseph Konrad (12 Nov 1905-23 Nov 2001)
68	ii.	Anna (8 May 1907-30 Jun 1977)
69	iii.	Maria (8 Apr 1909-1987)
70	iv.	Johannes (22 Jul 1912-)
71	v.	Dr. Med. Dent. Angela Aloysia (10 Dec 1904-8 Jun 1987)

Dr. Med. Den. Wilhelm Bernhard Valentin Thöne

38. Dr. Med. Den. Wilhelm Bernhard Valentin Thöne [1]. Born on 24 Aug 1893 in Düsseldorf. Wilhelm Bernhard Valentin died in 1957; he was 63.

This is the author of the book "Geschichte der Familie Thöne Warburger Stammes 1282-1938"

Else Link

On 29 Jul 1919 when Wilhelm Bernhard Valentin was 25, he married **Else Link**, daughter of Dr. Med. Matthias Link & Therese Payer (13 May 1897-).

They had the following children:

72	i.	Hildegunde (4 May 1920-)
73	ii.	Edeltraut Rosamunde (16 Sep 1921-)
74	iii.	Irmtrud (14 Oct 1922-)
75	iv.	Beatrix Giselinde (28 Oct 1929-)

Dr. Phil. Johannes Franz Seraph Thöne

39. Dr. Phil. Johannes Franz Seraph Thöne [1]. Born on 19 Nov 1884. Johannes Franz Seraph died in 1945; he was 60. Occupation: Priester, Oberelvenich (Voreifel).

Dr. Jur. Joseph Anton Thöne

40. Dr. Jur. Joseph Anton Thöne [1]. Born on 14 May 1887. Joseph Anton died in Verdun on 7 Oct 1916; he was 29. Occupation: Rechtsanwalt am Oberlandesgericht Düsseldorf.

Dr. Phil. Aloys Franz Anton Thöne

41. Dr. Phil. Aloys Franz Anton Thöne [1]. Born on 23 Sep 1888. Aloys Franz Anton died in 1967; he was 78. Occupation: Studienrat in Düsseldorf.

Maria Gertrud Thöne

42. Maria Gertrud Thöne [1]. Born on 21 May 1890. Maria Gertrud died in 1966; she was 75. Occupation: Ordensschwester.

Antonia Elisabeth Thöne

43. Antonia Elisabeth Thöne [1]. Born on 28 May 1896. Antonia Elisabeth died in 1952; she was 55. Occupation: Grundschullehrerin.

Anton Franz Xaver Thöne

44. Anton Franz Xaver Thöne [1]. Born on 14 May 1891. Anton Franz Xaver died on 22 Jun 1958; he was 67. Occupation: Pfarrer der Gemeinde St.-Josef, Essen-Katernberg.

Fifth Generation

Maria Klahold

45. Maria Klahold [9]. Born on 8 Aug 1911 in Paderborn. [3] Maria died in Paderborn on 10 Oct 1987; she was 76.

Maria married her cousin.

Eduard Hartmann

Maria married **Eduard Hartmann (57)** [9], son of Lorenz Hartmann (27) & Maria Catharina Stegemann (1892-1931). Born on 23 Jul 1917 in Wanne-Eickel. [10] Eduard died in Paderborn on 13 Jan 2001; he was 83. [10] Occupation: Schreiner.

Eduard married his cousin. He was active in the Kolpingwerkes in Paderborn (http://kolping-paderborn.de/)

Military: Eduard was a professional soldier. On January 1st 1936 he joined the Navy. He was first stationed at the III. Schiffsstammabteilung der Nordsee, Wesermünde. Next, he participated in the Spanish civil war on board the Kreuzer Köln (1937-1939). From December 17th, - August 18th 1943 he was stationed on the U-Boot "U 953". Since September 19th 1943 he was stationed at the 1. U-Ausbildungsabteilung, Plön. Next, he was registered from September 19th 1944 - December 18th 1944 at the 4. U-Flottille (ohne Bootsangabe). Since September 19th 1944 he was at the 6. Kriegsschiffbaulehrabteilung, Bremen; Baubelehrung für"U 3014". His last grade was "Obersteuermann". On August 12th, 1945 he was released from the British authorities with the registration U3014.

He received the "Spanienkreuz in Bronze" on June 6th 1939 and the "Medaille zur Erinnerung an den 01 .10.1938" on December 20th 1939.

They had one child:
    76   i.   Angelika Maria (21 Apr 1954-)

Anna Theresia Klahold

46. Anna Theresia Klahold. Anna Theresia died in Apr 2010; she was 97. Born on 18 Aug 1912 in Paderborn. [3]

Wilhelm Yacobius Stegemann

Anna Theresia married **Wilhelm Yacobius Stegemann**.

They had the following children:

77	i.	Gabriele Inge Elisabeth (21 May 1944-)
78	ii.	Wilfried (1 Jul 1950-)
79	iii.	Rainer (22 Mar 1941-)

Elisabeth Maria Klahold

47. Elisabeth Maria Klahold. Born on 10 Nov 1913. [11], [3] Elisabeth Maria died on 24 Apr 1993; she was 79. [11]

Wilhelm Leifeld

Elisabeth Maria married **Wilhelm Leifeld**. Wilhelm died on 31 Jul 2001; he was 90. [12] Born on 31 Oct 1910. [12]

They had the following children:
80	i.	Brigitte Elisabeth
81	ii.	Theresia (23 May 1947-20 Jul 2009)

Maria Wilhelmina Klahold

48. Maria Wilhelmina Klahold. Born on 9 Feb 1915 in Paderborn. [13], [3] Maria Wilhelmina died on 23 Dec 2001; she was 86. [13]

Christian Lorang

Maria Wilhelmina married **Christian Lorang**. Occupation: Koch.

They had the following children:

82	i.	Eduart Wilhelm (4 May 1951-)
83	ii.	Franz Joseph Antonius (9 Aug 1949-)
84	iii.	Peter August (11 Apr 1943-)
85	iv.	Maria Theresia (28 May 1941-)

Gertrud Johanna Klahold

49. Gertrud Johanna Klahold. Gertrud Johanna died in Paderborn on 19 May 1935; she was 19. [3] Born on 8 Mar 1916 in Paderborn. [3]

She died of Pneumonia after sun bathing on the cold ground. Penicillin was not yet available. Her coffin was decorated with Woodruff and she was the last of the family to be burried directly from her home to the cemetery. [14]

Johanna Christine Klahold

50. Johanna Christine Klahold. Born on 25 May 1917 in Paderborn. [3]

Johann Heinrich Hoppe

On 18 Aug 1943 when Johanna Christine was 26, she married **Johann Heinrich Hoppe**, son of Xaver Hoppe (1890-15 Jul 1952) & Therese Jakop, in Paderborn. Born on 31 Mar 1919 in Scherfede, Warburg, Höxter. Occupation: Lokführer. Address: Riemekehof, Pontanusstrasse 126, 33102 Paderborn.

Heinrich applied for membership in the NSDAP on October 23rd, 1938 and was accepted on September 1st, 1938 with the membership number 7016097. His membership card was issued on January 31st, 1939.

Military: Heinrich joined the army on September 20th, 1940. He served as an ambulance driver from 1941-1944. He was located in Drontheim (Norway). In 1944 he was send to the east front. [15]

Heinrich was captured by the Russian Army at the Sereth river, close to the Hungarian border, on September 6th, 1944. He appeared first in the Russian records as being placed in the hospital camp nr. 3006 in Drushkowka, Doneszk, Ukraine. From there, he was registered in the Russian camp (Gulag) nr, 217 and nr. 247 in the area of Doneszk, Ukraine. From his own recollection, he was imprisoned in Konstantinovka, Doneszk, Ukraine. [16]

Heinrich also filled in a KEG card in an attempt to receive a reimbursement for his time as a prisoner of war. He wrote in his application that he was in collecting camp Jassy in Rumania from September 6th, 1944 until December 3rd 1944. He was then in the camp Drushkowka 217/8 from December 10th 1944 until March 1947. From March 1947 until August 1949 he was in the camp Konstantinowka 242/7.

He was released from his imprisonment in the camp Gronefelde (Frankfurt an der Oder) on August 16th, 1949.

They had the following children:
86	i.	Wilhelmine Magdalena (28 Jul 1951-)
87	ii.	Ulrich Josef (10 Jul 1950-)

88   iii.   Wilhelm (23 Feb 1953-)

Theresia Henriette Klahold

51. Theresia Henriette Klahold. Born on 28 Dec 1918 in Paderborn. [17], [18], [3]

She is usually refered to as "Tante Resi".

52. Eduard Johannes Klahold. Born on 9 May 1920 in Paderborn. [3] Eduard Johannes died in Paderborn on 1 Jun 1920; he was <1. [3]

Josef Franz Klahold

53. Josef Franz Klahold. Born on 14 May 1921 in Paderborn. [3] Josef Franz died in Paderborn on 31 Mar 1937; he was 15.

Josef was killed by a train. It is not clear if it was murder, and accident or suicide. Josef did not want to join the Hitler Youth organization.

Franz Klahold

54. Franz Klahold. Franz died in Südwestlich Varna, Estland, on 2 Mar 1944; he was 21. Born on 22 Dec 1922 in Paderborn. [3]

The Bundesarchive has no NSDAP record of Franz. He died in the Second World War south of Varna in todays Estland. [3]

Military: Franz joined the army on October 9th, 1941. He served in Braunschweig, Leningrad, Oranienbaum and Narwa. He was killed by a shrapnel to his head and he is buried in the graveyard of the 170. Infrantie-Division in Toila (Estland). [15]

Heinrich Johannes Klahold

55. Heinrich Johannes Klahold. Born on 20 Feb 1924 in Paderborn. [3] Heinrich Johannes died in Paderborn on 10 Apr 2010; he was 86.

Theresia Menneken

Heinrich Johannes married **Theresia Menneken**. Address: Benediktinerstr. 68, 33098 Paderborn, Deutschland. Phone/FAX: +49525174108.

They had the following children:

89	i.	Thomas
90	ii.	Georg
91	iii.	Michael (-2009)

Angela Genoveva Klahold

56. Angela Genoveva Klahold. Born on 9 Apr 1926 in Paderborn. [3] Occupation: Krankenschwester. Address: Benediktinerstr. 68, 33098 Paderborn, Deutschland. Phone/FAX: +49525172303.

Eduard Hartmann

57. Eduard Hartmann [9]. Born on 23 Jul 1917 in Wanne-Eickel. [10] Eduard died in Paderborn on 13 Jan 2001; he was 83. [10] Occupation: Schreiner.

Eduard married his cousin. He was active in the Kolpingwerkes in Paderborn (http://kolping-paderborn.de/)

Military: Eduard was a professional soldier. On January 1st 1936 he joined the Navy. He was first stationed at the III. Schiffsstammabteilung der Nordsee, Wesermünde. Next, he participated in the Spanish civil war on board the Kreuzer Köln (1937-1939). From December 17th, - August 18th 1943 he was stationed on the U-Boot "U 953". Since September 19th 1943 he was stationed at the 1. U-Ausbildungsabteilung, Plön. Next, he was registered from September 19th 1944 - December 18th 1944 at the 4. U-Flottille (ohne Bootsangabe). Since September 19th 1944 he was at the 6. Kriegsschiffbaulehrabteilung, Bremen; Baubelehrung für"U 3014". His last grade was "Obersteuermann". On August 12th, 1945 he was released from the British authorities with the registration U3014.

He received the "Spanienkreuz in Bronze" on June 6th 1939 and the "Medaille zur Erinnerung an den 01 .10.1938" on December 20th 1939.

Maria Klahold

Eduard first married **Maria Klahold (45)** [9], daughter of Heinrich Klahold (13 Jul 1883-7 Mar 1965) & Theresia Hartmann (26) (3 Dec 1883-14 Mar 1965). Born on 8 Aug 1911 in Paderborn. [3] Maria died in Paderborn on 10 Oct 1987; she was 76.

Maria married her cousin.

They had one child:
  76   i.   Angelika Maria (21 Apr 1954-)

Charlotta Johanna Ingeborg Wunder

Eduard second married **Charlotta Johanna Ingeborg Wunder**. Born on 8 Jan 1923 in Hamburg. Charlotta Johanna Ingeborg died on 12 May 1997; she was 74.

from hamburg to london. married to british.

They had the following children:

92	i.	Uwe Eduard (1945-)
93	ii.	Marlies Wunder (17 Nov 1943-4 Feb 2004)

Franz Hartmann

58. Franz Hartmann. Born on 7 Aug 1924. Franz died on 20 Jun 1998; he was 73.

Maria Hesse

Franz married **Maria Hesse**, daughter of Bernhard Hesse & Anna Catharina Klüner. Born on 20 Jul 1927. Maria died on 23 Mar 1988; she was 60.

They had one child:

94	i.	Maria Elisabeth (15 Apr 1960-)

Johannes Hartmann

59. Johannes Hartmann. Born on 24 Nov 1919. Johannes died on 8 Aug 1998; he was 78.

Johannes was adopted by Stentrup to continue his work as a blacksmith. He therefore changed his name accordingly. He is know as "Hans Stentrup".

Maria

Johannes married **Maria**.

They had the following children:

95	i.	Wilhelm Stentrup
96	ii.	Johannes Lorenz Maria Stentrup
97	iii.	Joseph Stentrup (Twin)
98	iv.	Maria Stentrup (Twin)

Elisabeth Hartmann

60. Elisabeth Hartmann.

61. Gertrud Hartmann.

Died as a child.

62. Eduard Hesse.

Died in the war together with his brother.

63. Paula Hesse. Occupation: Schneiderin. Address: Giersstr. 1, 33098 Paderborn. Phone/FAX: +49525175867.

Child:

99	i.	Günther

64. Stefan Hesse.

65. Theresia Hesse.

66. Maria Hesse.

Maria married **August**.

They had the following children:

100	i.	Christa
101	ii.	Maria

Joseph Konrad Meiwes

67. Joseph Konrad Meiwes [19]. Born on 12 Nov 1905 in Paderborn. Joseph Konrad died in Gütersloh on 23 Nov 2001; he was 96.

On 14 Oct 1945 when Joseph Konrad was 39, he married **Karoline Meyer** [19], daughter of Karl Herman Johann Meyer & Anna Elisabeth Meschede, in Elsen, Paderborn. Born on 27 Jul 1920 in Oberntudorf, Salzkotten. Karoline died in Rietberg, Gütersloh, on 12 Jul 2009; she was 88.

They had the following children:

102	i.	Heinrich Christoph (20 Dec 1946-)
103	ii.	Karl Josef (11 Sep 1948-)
104	iii.	Hubertus Dyonisius (29 Jan 1951-)
105	iv.	Johannes Joachim (12 Jan 1953-)

Anna Meiwes

68. Anna Meiwes. Born on 8 May 1907. Anna died in Paderborn on 30 Jun 1977; she was 70.

Maria Meiwes

69. Maria Meiwes. Born on 8 Apr 1909. Maria died in 1987; she was 77.

Johannes Meiwes

70. Johannes Meiwes. Born on 22 Jul 1912 in Elsen, Paderborn.

Dr. Med. Dent. Angela Aloysia Meiwes

71. Dr. Med. Dent. Angela Aloysia Meiwes. Born on 10 Dec 1904. Angela Aloysia died in Paderborn on 8 Jun 1987; she was 82.

72. Hildegunde Thöne [1]. Born on 4 May 1920.

73. Edeltraut Rosamunde Thöne [1]. Born on 16 Sep 1921.

74. Irmtrud Thöne [1]. Born on 14 Oct 1922.

75. Beatrix Giselinde Thöne [1]. Born on 28 Oct 1929.

Sixth Generation
❖

76. A. M. Hartmann (Living, Female).

A. M. married **N. F. R. Wanless (Living, Male).**
They had the following children:
    106   i.   R. E. M. (Living, Male)

107   ii.   S. P. M. (Living, Female)

77. G. I. E. Stegemann (Living, Female).

G. I. E. married **A. Müller (Living, Male)**, son of Heinrich Müller & Elisabeth Hallman.
They had the following children:
    108   i.   D. W. (Living, Male)
    109   ii.   H. M. (Living, Female)

78. W. Stegemann (Living, Male).

W. first married **H. Adomeit (Living, Female)**.
W. second married **Monika**.
They had one child:
    110   i.   S. (Living, Male)

79. R. Stegemann (Living, Male).

Child:
    111   i.   T. (Living, Male)

80. B. E. Leifeld (Living, Female) [17].

B. E. married **F. W. G. Lüsse (Living, Male)** [17].
They had the following children:
    112   i.   B. U. (Living, Female)
    113   ii.   A. (Living, Male)
    114   iii.   R. (Living, Male)
    115   iv.   S. Goldapp (Living, Female)

Theresia Leifeld

81. Theresia Leifeld. Theresia died in Paderborn on 20 Jul 2009; she was 62. [18] Born on 23 May 1947 in Paderborn. [19]

82. E. W. Lorang (Living, Male).

E. W. married **U. Lagers (Living, Female)**, daughter of Eduart Lagers & Elisabeth Walter.
They had the following children:

116	i.	N. (Living, Female)
117	ii.	M. (Living, Female)

83. F. J. A. Lorang (Living, Male).

84. P. A. Lorang (Living, Male).

P. A. married **A. Temborius (Living, Female)**, daughter of Stefan Temborius & Theresia Röhren.
They had the following children:

118	i.	A. (Living, Male)
119	ii.	C. (Living, Female)

85. M. T. Lorang (Living, Female).

M. T. married **P. F. Kretschmer (Living, Male)**, son of Franz Kretschmer & Bertha Küssel.
They had one child:

120	i.	P. (Living, Male)

86. W. M. Hoppe (Living, Female).

W. M. married **K. D. Bartneck (Living, Male)**, son of Paul Wilhelm Bartneck (25 Nov 1909-7 Jul 1980) & Amalie Frieda Rother (17 Oct 1912-26 Sep 1981).
They had the following children:

121	i.	C. (Living, Male)
122	ii.	M. (Living, Male)

87. U. J. Hoppe (Living, Male).

U. J. married **U. Knocke (Living, Female)**, daughter of Rudolf Knocke (14 Sep 1915-5 Jul 1999) & Anni Gerold (6 Jun 1920-17 Jun 2007).
They had the following children:

123	i.	C. (Living, Female)

124   ii.   D. (Living, Female)

88. W. Hoppe (Living, Male).

W. married **K. M. E. Nell (Living, Female)**, daughter of Gerhard Nell (2 Oct 1932-25 Jul 1996) & R. Rother (Living, Female).
They had the following children:
    125   i.   S. (Living, Female)
    126   ii.   M. (Living, Male)

89. T. Klahold (Living, Male).

90. G. Klahold (Living, Male).

G. married **Claudia (Living, Female)**.
91. Michael Klahold. Born aft 1950. Michael died in 2009; he was 59.

92. U. E. Hartmann (Living, Male).

U. E. married **M. E. Kelly (Living, Female)**.
They had the following children:
    127   i.   A. E. (Living, Female)
    128   ii.   J. E. (Living, Male)

93. Marlies Wunder. Born on 17 Nov 1943. Marlies died in Hamburg on 4 Feb 2004; she was 60.

She was adopted in to her grand uncles family and changed her family name to Wunder. She was shortly married, but had no children.

94. M. E. Hartmann (Living, Female).

M. E. married **C. Koch (Living, Male)**.
They had the following children:
    129   i.   C. (Living, Female)
    130   ii.   C. (Living, Male)
    131   iii.   M. (Living, Male)

95. W. Stentrup (Living, Male).

W. married **Henriette Harvers**.
They had the following children:

132	i.	B. (Living, Male)
133	ii.	A. (Living, Male)
134	iii.	U. (Living, Female)

96. J. L. M. Stentrup (Living, Male).

J. L. M. married **Anette Wiggenbrock**.
97. J. Stentrup (Living, Male).

J. married **Barbara**.
They had the following children:

135	i.	M. (Living, Female)
136	ii.	S. (Living, Female)

98. M. Stentrup (Living, Female).

M. married **Johann Dunzig**.
They had the following children:

137	i.	A. (Living, Female)
138	ii.	T. (Living, Male)

99. Günther. Address: Hesse. Phone/FAX: +490525174431.

Children:

139	i.	Kathrin
140	ii.	Miriam

100. Christa.

101. Maria.

102. H. C. Meiwes (Living, Male) [16].

103. K. J. Meiwes (Living, Male) [16].

104. H. D. Meiwes (Living, Male) [16].

105. J. J. Meiwes (Living, Male) [16].

Seventh Generation

❖

106. R. E. M. Wanless (Living, Male).

R. E. M. married **A. Emmrich (Living, Female).**
They had one child:
    141   i.   E. (Living, Female)

107. S. P. M. Wanless (Living, Female).

S. P. M. married **R. A. Konersmann (Living, Male)**, son of Franz Josef
Alexander Konersmann & Brigitte Hingler.
They had one child:
    142   i.   T. (Living, Female)

108. D. W. Müller (Living, Male).

109. H. M. Müller (Living, Female).

H. M. married **R. Häser (Living, Male).**
They had the following children:
    143   i.   S. (Living, Female)
    144   ii.   V. (Living, Female)

110. S. Stegemann (Living, Male).

111. T. Stegemann (Living, Male).

112. B. U. Lüsse (Living, Female) [20].

B. U. married **K. Wiedemeier (Living, Male)** [20], son of Harald Herman
Wiedemeier & Margot Margarete Helene Schmalz.
They had the following children:
    145   i.   L. E. (Living, Female)
    146   ii.   M. (Living, Male)

113. A. Lüsse (Living, Male).

A. married **R. Hilker (Living, Female).**
114. R. Lüsse (Living, Male).

R. first married **Sibylle Kämper.**
They had the following children:

147	i.	L. Kämper (Living, Male)
148	ii.	M. Kämper (Living, Male)
149	iii.	S. Kämper (Living, Female)

R. second married **Christiane Gröpper**.
They had one child:

| 150 | i. | J. Gröpper (Living, Male) |

115. S. Goldapp (Living, Female).

Children:

| 151 | i. | V. Goldapp (Living, Female) |
| 152 | ii. | P. Goldapp (Living, Male) |

116. N. Lorang (Living, Female).

N. married **C. Schmidtmeier (Living, Male)**.
They had one child:

| 153 | i. | J. (Living, Male) |

117. M. Lorang (Living, Female).

118. A. Lorang (Living, Male).

A. married **S. Baumjohann (Living, Female)**.
They had one child:

| 154 | i. | J. (Living, Male) |

119. C. Lorang (Living, Female).

120. P. Kretschmer (Living, Male).

P. married **R. A. Auermann (Living, Female)**, daughter of Reinhold Josef
Auermann & Sigrid Helga Bilz.
They had one child:

| 155 | i. | S. (Living, Female) |

121. C. Bartneck (Living, Male).

C. married **A. あ. Masuoka 益岡 (Living, Female)**, daughter of T. 達.

Masuoka 益岡 (Living, Male) & E. 江. Hosokawa 細川 (Living, Female).

They had the following children:

156	i.	H. 花. (Living, Female)
157	ii.	S. 咲. (Living, Female)

122. M. Bartneck (Living, Male).

M. married **T. Herrmann (Living, Female)**, daughter of D. W. Herrmann (Living, Male) & B. Rottmann (Living, Female).
They had one child:

158	i.	M. (Living, Female)

123. C. Hoppe (Living, Female).

C. married **M. Bizer (Living, Male).**

124. D. Hoppe (Living, Female).

125. S. Hoppe (Living, Female).

S. married **E. Lickmeyer (Living, Male).**
They had the following children:

159	i.	L. (Living, Female)
160	ii.	K. (Living, Female)
161	iii.	F. (Living, Female)

126. M. Hoppe (Living, Male).

M. married **B. Drauschke (Living, Female).**

127. A. E. Hartmann (Living, Female).

128. J. E. Hartmann (Living, Male).

129. C. Koch (Living, Female).

130. C. Koch (Living, Male).

131. M. Koch (Living, Male).

132. B. Stentrup (Living, Male).

133. A. Stentrup (Living, Male).

134. U. Stentrup (Living, Female).

135. M. Stentrup (Living, Female).

136. S. Stentrup (Living, Female).

137. A. Dunzig (Living, Female).

138. T. Dunzig (Living, Male).

139. Kathrin.

140. Miriam.

Eighth Generation

141. E. Wanless (Living, Female).

142. T. Konersmann (Living, Female).

143. S. Häser (Living, Female).

144. V. Häser (Living, Female).

145. L. E. Wiedemeier (Living, Female).

146. M. Wiedemeier (Living, Male).

147. L. Kämper (Living, Male).

148. M. Kämper (Living, Male).

149. S. Kämper (Living, Female).

S. married **Christoph Gostonky.**
They had one child:
    162   i.   N. (Living, Male)

150. J. Gröpper (Living, Male).

151. V. Goldapp (Living, Female).

152. P. Goldapp (Living, Male).

153. J. Schmidtmeier (Living, Male).

154. J. Lorang (Living, Male).

155. S. Kretschmer (Living, Female).

156. H. 花. Bartneck (Living, Female).

157. S. 咲. Bartneck (Living, Female).

158. M. Bartneck (Living, Female).

159. L. Lickmeyer (Living, Female).

160. K. Lickmeyer (Living, Female).

161. F. Lickmeyer (Living, Female).

Ninth Generation

———— ❖ ————

162. N. Gostonky (Living, Male).

Sources

1. Dr. Wilhelm Thöne, "Geschichte Der Familie Thöne," 3, 1938.
2. <u>Kirchenbuch Paderborn Wewer, St. Johannes Baptist</u>, Diözesanarchiv Paderborn.
3. "Familienbuch Klahold Hartman."
4. "Sterbeurkunde Theresia Hartman," Standesamt Paderborn.
5. "Geburtsurkunde Theresia Hartmann."
6. "Heiratsurkunde Klahold Hartman," Standesamt Paderborn 9/1910.
7. "Geburtsurkunde Heinrich Klahold."
8. "Totenzettel Heinrich Klahold."
9. "Geburtsurkunde Angelika Maria Hartmann."
10. "Totenzettel Eduart Hartman."
11. "Totenzettel Elisabeth Maria Klahold."
12. "Totenzettel Wilhelm Leifeld."
13. "Totenzettel Maria Wilhelmina Klahold."

14. "Interiew with Angela Genoveva Klahold," January 24th, 2010, Christoph Bartneck, Phone.
15. "Deutsche Dienstelle," Jan 26th, 2011.
16. "Familienbuch Meiwes Meyer."
17. "Familienbuch Wedemeier Lüsse."
18. "Totenzettel Theresia Leifeld."
19. "Geburtsurkunde Theresia Leifeld."
20. "Abstammungsurkunde Lena Elisabeth Wiedemeier," Standesamt Paderborn.

Index

Anna Theodora (1822 -)   parent of spouse of 10

Claes
Anna Maria Elisabeth (1751 - 1814)   parent of spouse of 1

Dössing
Johann   parent of spouse of 24
Maria (1851 - 1914)   spouse of 24

Drewes
Conrad   spouse of 25
Franz Anton (1751 - 1789)   parent of spouse of 1
Maria Anna Juliana Antonette (1780 - 1846)   spouse of 1

Dunzig
Johann   spouse of 98

Gerold
Anni (1920 - 2007)   parent of spouse of 87

Gostonky
Christoph   spouse of 149

Graute
Heinrich   spouse of 18

Gröpper
Christiane   spouse of 114

Hallman
Elisabeth   parent of spouse of 77

Hapig
Anna Katharina (1798 - 1875)   parent of spouse of 6

Hartmann
Anna   25
Anna Bernardina (1841 - 1844)   11
Anna Theresia Wilhelmine (1857 -)   8
Bernard (1856 -)   12
Eduard (1917 - 2001)   spouse of 45
Eduard (1917 - 2001)   57
Elisabeth   60
Franciscus Antonius (Anton) (1806 - 1887)   spouse of 3
Franz   28
Franz (1924 - 1998)   58
Franz Josef   spouse of 2
Gertrud   61
Heinrich (1849 - 1908)   9
Johann Eduard (1846 - 1933)   10

Johannes	parent of spouse of 3
Johannes (1919 - 1998)	59
Kristiane	30
Lorenz	27
Lorenz	parent of spouse of 45
Maria	29
Maria Anna (1843 -)	13
Theresia (1883 - 1965)	26
Theresia (1883 - 1965)	parent of spouse of 57

Harvers

Henriette	spouse of 95

Hesse

Bernhard	parent of spouse of 58
Eduard	62
Josef	spouse of 30
Maria	66
Maria (1927 - 1988)	spouse of 58
Paula	63
Stefan	64
Theresia	spouse of 28
Theresia	65
unknown	parent of spouse of 28

Hingler

Brigitte	parent of spouse of 107

Hoppe

Xaver (1890 - 1952)	parent of spouse of 50

Jacobs

Franziska	parent of spouse of 24

Jakobs

Heinrich gen. Brockmeyer	spouse of 5

Jakop

Therese	parent of spouse of 50

Kämper

Sibylle	spouse of 114

Klahold

Anna Theresia (1912 - 2010)	46
Eduard Johannes (1920 - 1920)	52
Elisabeth Maria (1913 - 1993)	47
Franz (1846 - 1918)	parent of spouse of 26
Franz (1922 - 1944)	54

Gertrud Johanna (1916 - 1935) 49
Heinrich (1883 - 1965) spouse of 26
Heinrich (1883 - 1965) parent of spouse of 57
Heinrich Johannes (1924 - 2010) 55
Josef Franz (1921 - 1937) 53
Maria (1911 - 1987) 45
Maria (1911 - 1987) spouse of 57
Maria Wilhelmina (1915 - 2001) 48
Michael (>1950 - 2009) 91

Kloppenburg
Ludowika gen. Göke parent of spouse of 17

Klüner
Anna Catharina parent of spouse of 58

Knocke
Rudolf (1915 - 1999) parent of spouse of 87

Konersmann
Franz Josef Alexander parent of spouse of 107

Kretschmer
Franz parent of spouse of 85

Küssel
Bertha parent of spouse of 85

Lagers
Eduart parent of spouse of 82

Leifeld
Theresia (1947 - 2009) 81
Wilhelm (1910 - 2001) spouse of 47

Link
Else spouse of 38
Dr. Med. Matthias parent of spouse of 38

Lorang
Christian spouse of 48

Meier
Karl gen. Pulsen spouse of 19

Meiwes
Dr. Med. Dent. Angela Aloysia (1904 - 1987) 71
Anna (1907 - 1977) 68
Heinrich George (1886 - 1962) spouse of 37
Joseph Konrad (1905 - 2001) 67
Maria (1909 - 1987) 69

Meschede

Anna Elisabeth	parent of spouse of 67
Joseph gen. Kamp	parent of spouse of 17
Maria Ludowika (1849 - 1886)	spouse of 17

Meyer

Karl Herman Johann	parent of spouse of 67
Karoline (1920 - 2009)	spouse of 67

Müller

Heinrich	parent of spouse of 77

Nell

Gerhard (1932 - 1996)	parent of spouse of 88

Payer

Therese (1897 -)	parent of spouse of 38

Richter

Anna Maria (1820 - 1867)	spouse of 6
Joseph Conrad (1799 - 1860)	parent of spouse of 6

Röhren

Theresia	parent of spouse of 84

Rosendahl

Elisabeth (1890 - 1961)	spouse of 27

Rother

Amalie Frieda (1912 - 1981)	parent of spouse of 86

Schäfers

Johann (- 1866)	parent of spouse of 4
Theresia Gen. Mühlenburs (- 1866)	spouse of 4

Schmalz

Margot Margarete Helene	parent of spouse of 112

Steffens

Ludowika (1852 - 1928)	spouse of 23

Stegemann

Maria Catharina (1892 - 1931)	spouse of 27
Maria Catharina (1892 - 1931)	parent of spouse of 45
Wilhelm Yacobius	spouse of 46

Temborius

Stefan	parent of spouse of 84

Thöne

Dr. Phil. Aloys Franz Anton (1888 - 1967)	41
Aloysia Maria (1848 - 1907)	19

Anna Bernhardine (1841 -)   16
Anna Elisabeth (1858 -)   22
Anna Maria (1800 -)   7
Anna Maria Theresia (1808 - 1841)   5
Anna Maria Theresia (1813 - 1867)   3
Anton Franz Xaver (1891 - 1958)   44
Antonia Elisabeth (1896 - 1952)   43
Bernhard Gen. Mühlenburs (1810 - 1885)   4
Bernhard gen. Steffensmeier (1846 - 1928)   23
Bernhard (1874 - 1884)   33
Clemens August (1846 - 1853)   15
Franz (1886 - 1886)   36
Franz Seraph (1851 - 1906)   24
Johann Ferdinand gen. Stellbrink (1766 - 1813)   1
Johann Franz (1882 - 1884)   35
Johann Heinrich (1853 - 1926)   20
Johann Joseph (1872 - 1902)   32
Johann Jospeh (1870 - 1875)   31
Johannes Christophorus gen. Stellbrink (1803 - 1882)   6
Dr. Phil. Johannes Franz Seraph (1884 - 1945) 39
Dr. Jur. Joseph Anton (1887 - 1916)   40
Kaspar (1856 -)   21
Konrad Joseph gen. Stellbrink (1842 - 1909) 17
Maria Elisabeth (1805 -)   2
Maria Elisabeth Therese (1844 - 1848)   14
Maria Elisabeth Therese (1844 - 1908)   18
Maria Gertrud (1890 - 1966)   42
Maria Ludowika gen. Luise (1876 - 1957)   37
Theresia (1878 - 1898)   34
Dr. Med. Den. Wilhelm Bernhard Valentin (1893 - 1957)   38

Walter
Elisabeth   parent of spouse of 82

Westermeyer
Maria Theodora   parent of spouse of 3

Wiedemeier
Harald Herman   parent of spouse of 112

Wiggenbrock
Anette   spouse of 96

Wunder
Charlotta Johanna Ingeborg (1923 - 1997)   spouse of 57
Marlies (1943 - 2004)   93

The Thöne Ancestors

First Generation

—— ❖ ——

1 Johann Ferdinand Thöne gen. Stellbrink. [1] Johann Ferdinand died in Paderborn-Wewer, Paderborn, on 21 Apr 1813; he was 47. Born on 20 Jan 1766 in Altenbeken, Paderborn. Occupation: Vollmeier.

On 26 Sep 1800 when Johann Ferdinand was 34, he married **Maria Anna Juliana Antonette Drewes**. [2]

They had the following children:
i.	Maria Elisabeth (1805-)
ii.	Anna Maria Theresia (1813-1867)
iii.	Bernhard Gen. Mühlenburs (1810-1885)
iv.	Anna Maria Theresia (1808-1841)
v.	Johannes Christophorus gen. Stellbrink [1] (1803-1882)

maybe he did not die in 1813, because a child of his was born that year. Or maybe he died not in Wewer. The Wewever death registry did not have an entry for him.

Second Generation

—— ❖ ——

2 Johann Christoph Thöne gen. Holschenwirt. [1] Born on 14 Sep 1738 in Kempen, Viersen. Johann Christoph died in Paderborn-Altenbeken, Paderborn, on 30 Apr 1823; he was 84. Occupation: Vollmeier und Gastwirt in Altenbecken.

On 5 Nov 1765 when Johann Christoph was 27, he married **Maria Katharina Eckebracht** [1].

They had the following children:

54

1	i.	Johann Ferdinand gen. Stellbrink (1766-1813)
	ii.	Johann Ferdinand gen. Johann [1] (1768-1808)
	iii.	Maria Angela [1] (1771-1846)
	iv.	Johann Jürgen [1] (1774-1840)

3 Maria Katharina Eckebracht. [1] Maria Katharina died on 10 Jun 1774.

Third Generation
————— ✛ —————

4 Johann Heinrich Thöne. [1] Born on 16 Feb 1710 in Paderborn-Dören, Paderborn. Johann Heinrich died in Bad Lippspringe, Paderborn, on 26 Sep 1783; he was 73. (Could also be 29 Jul 1783).

Child:

| 2 | i. | Johann Christoph gen. Holschenwirt (1738-1823) |

6 Ferdinand Eckebracht. [1] Occupation: Holschenwirtes.

Ferdinand married **Theresia Rodefeld** [1].

They had one child:

| 3 | i. | Maria Katharina (-1774) |

7 Theresia Rodefeld. [1]

Fourth Generation
————— ✛ —————

8 Georg Thöne. [1] Born on 14 Apr 1669 in Bad Driburg-Herste, Höxter. Georg died in Paderborn on 18 Nov 1729; he was 60.

On 5 Apr 1697 when Georg was 27, he married **Elisabeth Hoeken** [1] in Brakel-Bellersen, Höxter.

They had the following children:

4	i.	Johann Heinrich (1710-1783)
	ii.	Wilhelm [1] (1692-)
	iii.	Franz Jürgen [1] (1695-)
	iv.	Hermann [1] (1698-1739)

v.	Anna Maria [1] (1700-)
vi.	Jobst [1] (1702-)
vii.	Anna Elisabeth [1] (1712-)
viii.	Johann Georg

9 Elisabeth Hoeken. [1]

Fifth Generation

---------- ❖ ----------

16 Wilhelm I. Thöne. Born in 1630 in Borgentreich-Körbecke, Höxter.

In 1650 when Wilhelm I. was 20, he married **Katharina Teves** [1] in Bad Driburg-Herste, Höxter.

They had the following children:

8	i.	Georg (1669-1729)
	ii.	Katharina [1] (1655-)
	iii.	Margareta [1] (1660-1704)
	iv.	Christian [1] (1665-1746)
	v.	Dirk [1] (1670-)
	vi.	Wilhelm II. [1] (1682-)
	vii.	Jobst (Joducus) [1] (1652-1722)
	viii.	Gertrud [1] (-1691)
	ix.	Maria [1] (1658-)
	x.	Liborius [1] (1663-1739)
	xi.	Anna Margareta [1] (1674-1760)

17 Katharina Teves. [1] Katharina died on 9 Feb 1683 in Brakel-Hainhausen, Höxter.

Sixth Generation

---------- ❖ ----------

32 Johann II. Thöne. [1] Born in 1595 in Warburg, Höxter. Johann II. died in Warburg, Höxter, in 1643; he was 48.

Ratsherr zu Warburg, von Cansteinscher Meier in Cörbecke 1627-1632, Vogt und Zolleinnehmer zu Germete 1637

In 1615 when Johann II. was 20, he married **N. Brabant**.

They had the following children:

16	i.	Wilhelm I. (1630-)
	ii.	Clara [1] (1616-1685)
	iii.	N. [1]
	iv.	Curd [1] (1620-)
	v.	Philipp (Lips) [1] (1629-1699)

33 N. Brabant.

Seventh Generation

64 Johan I. Thöne. [1] Born in 1570 in Warburg, Höxter. Johan I. died in Warburg, Höxter, in 1618; he was 48. Occupation: Von Cantsteiner Vogt un Meier 1613-1618.

Children:

32	i.	Johann II. (1595-1643)
	ii.	Thomas II. [1] (1590-1639)

66 Franz Brabant. [1]

Child:

33	i.	N.

Eighth Generation

128 Thomas I. Thöne. [1] Born in 1550 in Warburg, Höxter. Thomas I. died in Warburg, Höxter. Occupation: Von Cansteischer Vogt und Meier zu Germete 1573-1577.

Child:

64	i.	Johan I. (1570-1618)

Ninth Generation
———————— ✣ ————————

256 Jost II. Junior Thöne. [1] Born in Warburg, Höxter. Jost II. Junior died in 1581 in Warburg, Höxter. Occupation: Ratsherr in Pappenheim 1552-1580, Meier in Germete.

Build the house on the Rotthofe in 1578

In 1550 Jost II. Junior married **Ilse**.

They had the following children:

128	i.	Thomas I. (1550-)
	ii.	Heinrich III. [1]
	iii.	Cord V. [1]
	iv.	Gertrud

257 Ilse. Born in Zierenberg.

Tenth Generation
———————— ✣ ————————

512 Heinrich II. Thöne. [1] Born in Warburg, Höxter. Heinrich II. died in Warburg, Höxter. Occupation: Ratsherr in Mohlhausen 1523-1579, Meier in Germete.

In 1552 Heinrich II. married **Anna** [1].

They had the following children:

256	i.	Jost II. Junior (-1581)
	ii.	Hermann III. [1]
	iii.	Else [1]

513 Anna. [1] Born in Warburg, Höxter. Anna died in Warburg, Höxter.

Eleventh Generation
———————— ✣ ————————

1024 Johann II. Thöne. [1] Born in Warburg, Höxter. Johann II. died in Warburg, Höxter.

In 1500 Johann II. married **N. Giseler** [1].

They had the following children:
   512   i.   Heinrich II.
             ii.   Cord III. [1] (1518-1554)
             iii.   Giseler I. [1] (1526-1566)

1025 N. Giseler. [1] Born in Warburg, Höxter. N. died in Warburg, Höxter.

Twelfth Generation

—✤—

2048 Cord II. Thöne. [1] Born in Warburg, Höxter. Cord II. died in Warburg, Höxter.

1474-1517 in Papenheim

Child:
  1024   i.   Johann II.

2050 Heinrich Giseler. [1] Occupation: Bürgermeister.

Child:
  1025   i.   N.

Thirteenth Generation

—✤—

4096 Johann I. Thöne. [1] Born in Warburg, Höxter. Johann I. died in Warburg, Höxter.

In Busdorf in 1464

Children:
  2048   i.   Cord II.
            ii.   Hermann II. [1]

iii.   Volmar [1]

14th Generation

—————— ❖ ——————

8192 Cord I. Thöne. [1] Born in 1410 in Warburg, Höxter. Cord I. died in Warburg, Höxter. Occupation: Ratsherr.

Living in Busdorf

Children:
4096   i.   Johann I.
        ii.   Hermann I.

15th Generation

—————— ❖ ——————

16384 Johann II. Thöne. [1] Born ca 1350 in Warburg, Höxter. Occupation: 1422 Ratsherr der Warburg Altstadt.

Children:
        i.   Johann III. [1] (ca1400-)
8192   ii.   Cord I. (1410-)

16th Generation

—————— ❖ ——————

32768 Johann I. Thöne. [1] Born ca 1322 in Warburg, Höxter. Occupation: 1347 Ratsherr der Warburg Altstadt.

ca 1348 when Johann I. was 26, he married **Regenheidis** [1].

They had one child:
16384   i.   Johann II. (ca1350-)

32769 Regenheidis. [1]

17th Generation

———————— ✣ ————————

65536 Cord I. Thöne. [1] Born ca 1300 in Warburg, Höxter. Cord I. died in Warburg, Höxter, in 1359; he was 59. Occupation: Ratsherr der Warbug Altstadt.

Children:

32768	i.	Johann I. (ca1322-)
	ii.	Hermann III. [1] (ca1320-)
	iii.	Heinrich I. [1] (ca1325-1381)

18th Generation

———————— ✣ ————————

131072 Hermann II. Thöne. [1] Born ca 1275 in Warburg, Höxter. Occupation: 1331 Vorsteher der Wollweber.

Child:

| 65536 | i. | Cord I. (ca1300-1359) |

19th Generation

———————— ✣ ————————

262144 Hermann I. Thuno gen. Thonaman. [1] Born in Warburg, Höxter. Occupation: 1282 Ratsherr der Warburg Altstadt.

Child:

| 131072 | i. | Hermann II. (ca1275-) |

Sources

1. Dr. Wilhelm Thöne, "Geschichte Der Familie Thöne," 3, 1938.
2. Kirchenbuch Paderborn Wewer, St. Johannes Baptist, Diözesanarchiv Paderborn.

Index

Anna	513
Ilse	257

Brabant

Franz	66
N.	33

Drewes

Maria Anna Juliana Antonette (1780 - 1846)	spouse of 1

Eckebracht

Ferdinand	6
Maria Katharina (- 1774)	3

Giseler

Heinrich	2050
N.	1025

Hoeken

Elisabeth	9

Regenheidis

UNNAMED	32769

Rodefeld

Theresia	7

Teves

Katharina (- 1683)	17

Thöne

Anna Elisabeth (1712 -)	child of 8
Anna Margareta (1674 - 1760)	child of 16
Anna Maria (1700 -)	child of 8
Anna Maria Theresia (1808 - 1841)	child of 1
Anna Maria Theresia (1813 - 1867)	child of 1
Bernhard Gen. Mühlenburs (1810 - 1885)	child of 1
Christian (1665 - 1746)	child of 16
Clara (1616 - 1685)	child of 32
Cord I. (ca1300 - 1359)	65536
Cord I. (1410 -)	8192
Cord II.	2048
Cord III. (1518 - 1554)	child of 1024
Cord V.	child of 256
Curd (1620 -)	child of 32
Dirk (1670 -)	child of 16
Else	child of 512

Franz Jürgen (1695 -)	child of 8	
Georg (1669 - 1729)	8	
Gertrud (- 1691)	child of 16	
Gertrud	child of 256	
Giseler I. (1526 - 1566)	child of 1024	
Heinrich I. (ca1325 - 1381)	child of 65536	
Heinrich II.	512	
Heinrich III.	child of 256	
Hermann (1698 - 1739)	child of 8	
Hermann I.	child of 8192	
Hermann II.	child of 4096	
Hermann II. (ca1275 -)	131072	
Hermann III.	child of 512	
Hermann III. (ca1320 -)	child of 65536	
Jobst (1702 -)	child of 8	
Jobst (Joducus) (1652 - 1722)	child of 16	
Johan I. (1570 - 1618)	64	
Johann Christoph gen. Holschenwirt (1738 - 1823)	2	
Johann Ferdinand gen. Stellbrink (1766 - 1813)	1	
Johann Ferdinand gen. Johann (1768 - 1808)	child of 2	
Johann Georg	child of 8	
Johann Heinrich (1710 - 1783)	4	
Johann I.	4096	
Johann I. (ca1322 -)	32768	
Johann II.	1024	
Johann II. (ca1350 -)	16384	
Johann II. (1595 - 1643)	32	
Johann III. (ca1400 -)	child of 16384	
Johann Jürgen (1774 - 1840)	child of 2	
Johannes Christophorus gen. Stellbrink (1803 - 1882)		child of 1
Jost II. Junior (- 1581)	256	
Katharina (1655 -)	child of 16	
Liborius (1663 - 1739)	child of 16	
Margareta (1660 - 1704)	child of 16	
Maria (1658 -)	child of 16	
Maria Angela (1771 - 1846)	child of 2	
Maria Elisabeth (1805 -)	child of 1	
N.	child of 32	
Philipp (Lips) (1629 - 1699)	child of 32	
Thomas I. (1550 -)	128	
Thomas II. (1590 - 1639)	child of 64	
Volmar	child of 4096	

Wilhelm (1692 -)	child of 8
Wilhelm I. (1630 -)	16
Wilhelm II. (1682 -)	child of 16

Thuno

Hermann I. gen. Thonaman	262144

The Drewes Ancestors

First Generation

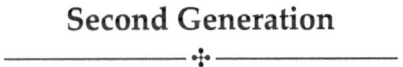

1 Maria Anna Juliana Antonette Drewes. Born on 3 Dec 1780 in Kempen, Viersen. Maria Anna Juliana Antonette died in Paderborn-Wewer, Paderborn, on 17 Dec 1846; she was 66.

On 26 Sep 1800 when Maria Anna Juliana Antonette was 19, she married **Johann Ferdinand Thöne gen. Stellbrink** [1]. [2]

They had the following children:

i.	Maria Elisabeth (1805-)
ii.	Anna Maria Theresia (1813-1867)
iii.	Bernhard Gen. Mühlenburs (1810-1885)
iv.	Anna Maria Theresia (1808-1841)
v.	Johannes Christophorus gen. Stellbrink [1] (1803-1882)

maybe he did not die in 1813, because a child of his was born that year. Or maybe he died not in Wewer. The Wewever death registry did not have an entry for him.

Second Generation

2 Franz Anton Drewes. [1] Born on 28 Oct 1751 in Steinheim-Sandebeck, Höxter. Franz Anton died in Kempen, Viersen, on 21 Nov 1789; he was 38. Occupation: Vollmeier.

On 24 Apr 1777 when Franz Anton was 25, he married **Anna Maria Elisabeth Claes** [1].

They had one child:

    1   i.   Maria Anna Juliana Antonette (1780-1846)

3 Anna Maria Elisabeth Claes. [1] Born on 28 Oct 1751 in Kempen, Viersen. Anna Maria Elisabeth died on 2 Jun 1814; she was 62.

Third Generation
— ❖ —

4 Anton Bernhard Drewes. [1] Born on 13 Feb 1720 in Steinheim-Sandebeck, Höxter. Anton Bernhard died in Steinheim-Sandebeck, Höxter, on 7 Dec 1763; he was 43. Occupation: Freier Bauer.

On 23 Jul 1745 when Anton Bernhard was 25, he married **Katharina Maria Von Bose** [1].

They had one child:

    2   i.   Franz Anton (1751-1789)

5 Katharina Maria Von Bose. [1] Born on 24 Mar 1705 in Steinheim-Sandebeck, Höxter. Katharina Maria died in Steinheim-Sandebeck, Höxter, on 4 Apr 1758; she was 53.

Fourth Generation
— ❖ —

10 Everhard Wilhelm Von Bose. [1] Born in Feb 1655 in Paderborn. Everhard Wilhelm died in Steinheim-Sandebeck, Höxter, on 5 Mar 1710; he was 55. Occupation: Vogt zu Sandebeck.

On 18 Mar 1700 when Everhard Wilhelm was 45, he married **Maria Helling** [1].

They had one child:

    5   i.   Katharina Maria (1705-1758)

11 Maria Helling. [1] Born in Vlotho, Herford.

Fifth Generation

————————— ✥ —————————

20 Franz Dietrich Von Bose. [3] Born in 1690. Occupation: Herr zu Pömbsen. **Start of the Bose line.**

Franz Dietrich married **Sibilla Wigand** [3].

They had one child:
    10   i.   Everhard Wilhelm (1655-1710)

21 Sibilla Wigand. [3]

22 Caspar Cornelius Helling. [1] Caspar Cornelius died on 7 Aug 1695 in Vlotho, Herford. Occupation: Amtmann.

ca 1650 Caspar Cornelius married **Hedewig Von Der Horst** [1].

They had one child:
    11   i.   Maria

23 Hedewig Von Der Horst. [1] Hedewig died bef 1693. **Start of the Horst line.**

Sixth Generation

————————— ✥ —————————

40 George Von Bose. Occupation: Oberstleutnant (1640-1652), Herr zu Pömbsen.

George married **Elisabeth Margarethe von Wesphalen zu Herbram** [3].

They had one child:
    20   i.   Franz Dietrich (1690-)

41 Elisabeth Margarethe von Wesphalen zu Herbram. [3]

46 Arnold Von Der Horst. [1], [4] Arnold died in 1641. Occupation: Droste zu Vlotho.

He is named on the Wittekindstein in Vlotho, Bonneberg.

Arnold married **Anna Margareta Von Rüspe** [1].

They had one child:

23	i.	Hedewig (-<1693)

47 Anna Margareta Von Rüspe. [1] Anna Margareta died aft 1641.

Seventh Generation
———————— ❖ ————————

82 Bernhard von Wesphalen zu Herbram. [3] Born in 1648. Bernhard died in 1682; he was 34.

Bernhard married **Eva Dorothea von Ense** [3].

They had one child:

41	i.	Elisabeth Margarethe

83 Eva Dorothea von Ense. [3]

94 Christoph Von Rüspe zu Brüninghausen. [1] Christoph died on 19 Dec 1614.

In 1597 Christoph married **Sybilla Von Efferen** [1].

They had one child:

47	i.	Anna Margareta (->1641)

95 Sybilla Von Efferen. [1]

Eighth Generation
———————— ❖ ————————

166 Walther Philipp von Ense zu Westkotten. [3] Born in 1628.

Walther Philipp married **Katharina von Hörde zu Störmede und Ehringerfeld**.

They had one child:

83   i.   Eva Dorothea

167 Katharina von Hörde zu Störmede und Ehringerfeld.

190 Adolf Von Efferen zu Disternich. [1] Born in 1549. Adolf died bef 1582; he was 33.

Adolf married **Margarete Von Bernsau zum Hardeberg.**

They had one child:
    95   i.   Sybilla

191 Margarete Von Bernsau zum Hardeberg.

Ninth Generation

332 Heinrich von Ense. [3] Heinrich died on 1 Nov 1592. Occupation: Drost zu Stromberg.

Heinrich married **Theodora von Büren** [3].

They had one child:
    166   i.   Walther Philipp (1628-)

333 Theodora von Büren. [3] Occupation: Edle.

382 Wilhelm Von Bernsau zum Hardeberg. [1] Wilhelm died in 1572. Occupation: Bergischer Rat und Marschall, Amtmann zu Solingern.

In 1542 Wilhelm married **Anna Von Plettenberg zu Schönrad** [1].

They had one child:
    191   i.   Margarete

383 Anna Von Plettenberg zu Schönrad. [1]

Tenth Generation

666 Johann Edelherr von Büren. [3] Johann died in 1592. Occupation: Oberfeldherr des westfälischen Kreises.

Johann married **Mathilde von Hörde zu Schwarzengraben** [3].

They had one child:
    333   i.   Theodora

667 Mathilde von Hörde zu Schwarzengraben. [3]

766 Dietrich Von Plettenberg zu Schönrad. [1] Dietrich died in 1521.

In 1503 Dietrich married **Barbera Scheiffart Von Merode zu Bornheim** [1].

They had one child:
    383   i.   Anna

767 Barbera Scheiffart Von Merode zu Bornheim. [1]

Eleventh Generation

1332 Bernhard von Büren. [3] Bernhard died in 1551. Occupation: Edelherr.

Bernhard married **Alfradis von Wrede zu Mylinghausen** [3].

They had one child:
    666   i.   Johann (-1592)

1333 Alfradis von Wrede zu Mylinghausen. [3]

1532 Bertold Von Plettenberg zu Schönrad. [1] Born in 1444. Bertold died in 1477; he was 33. Occupation: Hofmeister des Herzogs Gert von Jülich.

Bertold married **Irmgrad von Nesselrode-Stein** [1].

They had one child:
    766   i.   Dietrich (-1521)

1533 Irmgrad von Nesselrode-Stein. [1]

Twelfth Generation

—————— ✣ ——————

2664 Johann von Büren. [3] Johann died in 1481. Occupation: Edelherr.

Johann married **N. Wolf von Gudenberg.**

They had one child:
1332   i.   Bernhard (-1551)

2665 N. Wolf von Gudenberg. N. Wolf died in 1484.

3066 Johann von Nesselrode-Stein. [1] Born in 1442. Johann died in 1498; he was 56. Occupation: Bergischer Landdrost und Amtmann zu Elberfeld.

Johann married **Katharina Von Gemen** [1].

They had one child:
1533   i.   Irmgrad

3067 Katharina Von Gemen. [1] Born in 1442. Katharina died in 1496; she was 54.

Thirteenth Generation

—————— ✣ ——————

5328 Bernhard von Büren. [3] Born in 1443. Bernhard died in 1478; he was 35. Occupation: Edelherr.

Bernhard married **Willa von Wesphalen zu Fürstenberg** [3].

They had one child:
2664   i.   Johann (-1481)

5329 Willa von Wesphalen zu Fürstenberg. [3] Born in 1426.

6134 Johann Von Gemen. [1] Born in 1405. Johann died in 1455; he was 50. Occupation: Edelherr, Rat des Herzogs von Geldern.

Johann married **Oda Von Horn.**

They had one child:
    3067   i.   Katharina (1442-1496)

6135 Oda Von Horn.

14th Generation

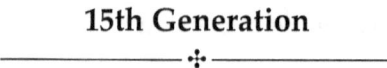

10656 Wilhelm von Büren-Davensberg. [3] Occupation: Edelherr.

ca 1365 Wilhelm married **Margaretha von Sayn-Wittgenstein** [3].

They had one child:
    5328   i.   Bernhard (1443-1478)

10657 Margaretha von Sayn-Wittgenstein. [3] Occupation: Gräfin.

12270 Wilhelm Von Horn. [1] Born in 1377. Wilhelm died in bei Acincourt, on 25 Oct 1455; he was 78. Occupation: Edlelherr von Horn, Herr zu Altena, Werth und Cranenburg, Erbgrossjägermeister des Reiches.

Wilhelm married **Dorothea Von Loos** [1].

They had one child:
    6135   i.   Oda

12271 Dorothea Von Loos. [1]

15th Generation

21314 Salentin von Sayn-Wittgenstein. [3] Born in 1340. Salentin died in 1386; he was 46. Occupation: Graf.

bef 1345 when Salentin was 5, he married **Adelheid von Wittgenstein** [3].

They had one child:
    10657   i.   Margaretha

21315 Adelheid von Wittgenstein. [3] Occupation: Gräfin.

24542 Gottfried Graf Von Loos. [1] Born in 1357. Gottfried Graf died in 1395; he was 38. Occupation: Herr zu Heinsberg und Dalenbrock.

Gottfried Graf married **Philippa Von Jülich** [1].

They had one child:
   12271   i.   Dorothea

24543 Philippa Von Jülich. [1] Philippa died bef 1350.

16th Generation
❖

42628 Gottfried von Sayn. [3] Born in 1324. Gottfried died in 1354; he was 30. Occupation: Graf, Herr zu Homburg und Vallendar.

Gottfried married **Sophie von Vomarstein** [3].

They had one child:
   21314   i.   Salentin (1340-1386)

42629 Sophie von Vomarstein. [3] Occupation: Edle.

49086 Wilhelm V. Von Jülich. [1] Born ca 1317. Wilhelm V. died in 1361; he was 44. Occupation: Graf und Herzog zu Jülich.

On 26 Feb 1324 when Wilhelm V. was 7, he married **Johanna Von Holland** [1]. [5]

They had the following children:
24543	i.	Philippa (-<1350)
	ii.	Richardis [6]
	iii.	Gerhard VI. [6] (-1360)
	iv.	Johanna [6] (-<1367)
	v.	Wilhelm II. [6] (ca1325-1393)
	vi.	Isabella [6] (-1411)

49087 Johanna Von Holland. [1] Born in 1315. [5] Johanna died in 1374; she was 59.

Tafel 49

17th Generation

85258 Dietrich I. von Volmarstein. [3] Born in 1250. Dietrich I. died in 1314; he was 64. Occupation: Edelherr.

Dietrich I. married **Kunigunde von Dormund** [3].

They had one child:
  42629   i.   Sophie

85259 Kunigunde von Dormund. [3] Occupation: Burggräfin.

98172 Gerhard V. Von Jülich. [1] Born in 1279. Gerhard V. died on 29 Jul 1328; he was 49. Occupation: Graf von Jülich.

Gerhard V. married **Elisabeth Von Brabant** [1].

They had the following children:
  49086   i.   Wilhelm V. (ca1317-1361)
               ii.   Marie [6] (-1353)
               iii.   Elisabeth [6]
               iv.   Heinrich [6] (1319-1334)
               v.   Richardis [6] (-<1355)
               vi.   Walram [6] (1322-1349)
               vii.   Gottfried [6] (-1335)

98173 Elisabeth Von Brabant. [1] Born in 1303. Elisabeth died bef 1350; she was 47. Occupation: Gräfin von Aerschot.

18th Generation

170516 Heinrich III von Volmarstein. [3] Born in 1209. Heinrich III died in 1250; he was 41. Occupation: Edelherr.

Heinrich III married **Sophie von Isenburg** [3].

74

They had one child:

85258	i.	Dietrich I. (1250-1314)

170517 Sophie von Isenburg. [3] Occupation: Gräfin.

196346 Gottfried Von Brabant. [1] Born ca 1267. Gottfried died on 11 Jul 1302; he was 35. Occupation: Graf von Aerschot.

In 1280 when Gottfried was 13, he married **Johanna Von Vierson und Mesiers** [1].

They had the following children:

98173	i.	Elisabeth (1303-<1350)
	ii.	Johann [6] (1281-1302)
	iii.	Maria [6] (-1330)
	iv.	Alix [7] (-1315)
	v.	Blanche [6] (-1329)
	vi.	Margarete [6] (->1318)
	vii.	Johanna [6] (->1318)

196347 Johanna Von Vierson und Mesiers. [1]

19th Generation

———————— ❖ ————————

341034 Friedrich von Isenburg. [3] Born bef 1193. Friedrich died on 14 Nov 1226; he was 33. Occupation: Graf, Altena und Nienbrügge.

Friedrich married **Sophie von Limburg** [3].

They had the following children:

170517	i.	Sophie
	ii.	Dietrich [6] (ca1215-1301)
	iii.	Friedrich [6]
	iv.	Agnes [6]
	v.	Elisabeth [6]

341035 Sophie von Limburg. [3] Sophie died in 1226. Occupation: Herzogin.

Heinrich III. Der Friedfertige Von Brabant

392692 Heinrich III. Der Friedfertige Von Brabant. [1] Born ca 1231. Heinrich III. Der Friedfertige died on 28 Feb 1261; he was 30. Occupation: Herzog von Brabant.

ca 1251 when Heinrich III. Der Friedfertige was 20, he married **Adelheid Von Burgund** [1].

They had the following children:

196346	i.	Gottfried (ca1267-1302)
	ii.	Heinrich IV. [6] (1251-1272)
	iii.	Johan I. der Siegreiche [6] (1253-1294)
	iv.	Maria [6] (1256-1321)

392693 Adelheid Von Burgund. [1] Born in 1233. Adelheid died on 23 Oct 1273; she was 40.

20th Generation

✛

682070 Walram IV. von Limburg. [3] Born in 1198. Walram IV. died in 1226; he was 28. Occupation: Herzog, Graf von Luxemburg, Markgraf von Arlon.

Military: Walram participated in the third crusade together with his father.

Walram IV. married **Kunigunde von Monschau** [3].

They had the following children:

341035	i.	Sophie (-1226)
	ii.	Mathilde [6]
	iii.	Heinrich IV. [6] (-1247)
	iv.	Walram II. [6] (-1242)

682071 Kunigunde von Monschau. [3] Occupation: Gräfin.

Heinrich II. der Grossmütige Von Brabant

785384 Heinrich II. der Grossmütige Von Brabant. [1] Born in 1207. Heinrich II. der Grossmütige died on 1 Feb 1248; he was 41. Occupation: Herzog von Brabant.

On 22 Aug 1215 when Heinrich II. der Grossmütige was 8, he married **Maria Von Hohenstaufen** [1].

They had the following children:

392692	i.	Heinrich III. Der Friedfertige (ca1231-1261)
	ii.	Philip [6]
	iii.	Mathilde [6] (1224-1288)
	iv.	Beatrix [6] (1225-1288)
	v.	Maria [6] (ca1226-1256)
	vi.	Margarethe [6] (-1277)

785385 Maria Von Hohenstaufen. [1] Maria died in 1235.

785386 Hugo IV Von Burgund. Occupation: Herzog von Burgund.

Child:

392693	i.	Adelheid (1233-1273)

21st Generation

❖

1364140 Heinrich III. von Limburg. [3] Born ca 1140. Heinrich III. died on 21 Jun 1221; he was 81. Occupation: Herzog, Graf von Luxemburg, Markgraf von Arlon.

Heinrich III. married **Sophie von Lothringen** [3].

They had the following children:
682070	i.	Walram IV. (1198-1226)
	ii.	Heinrich IV. [6] (ca1165-1214)
	iii.	Friederich [6]
	iv.	Gerhard II. [6] (-1225)
	v.	Simon [6] (1178-1195)
	vi.	Judith [6] (-1202)
	vii.	Macharius [6]
	viii.	Isabella [6] (-1221)

1364141 Sophie von Lothringen. [3] Born ca 1149. Sophie died aft 1215; she was 66. Occupation: Herzogin.

Philipp Von Schwaben

1570770 Philipp Von Schwaben. [1] Born ca 1178. Philipp died on 21 Jun 1208; he was 30. Occupation: Deutscher König.

On 25 May 1197 when Philipp was 19, he married **Irene Marie Von Byzanz** [1].

They had the following children:
785385	i.	Maria (-1235)
	ii.	Beatrix [6] (1198-1212)
	iii.	Kunigunde [6] (1200-1248)
	iv.	Elisabeth [6] (1203-1235)
	v.	Rainald [6]
	vi.	Friedrich [6] (1206-)

vii.   Beatrix Posthuma [6] (1208-)

1570771 Irene Marie Von Byzanz. [1] Born ca 1177. Irene Marie died on 27 Aug 1208; she was 31.

22nd Generation

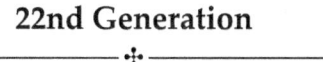

2728280 Heinrich II. von Limburg. [3] Born ca 1110. Heinrich II. died on 19 Aug 1167; he was 57. Occupation: Herzog.

Heinrich II. married **Mathilde von Saffenberg** [3].

They had one child:
1364140   i.   Heinrich III. (ca1140-1221)

2728281 Mathilde von Saffenberg. [3] Born ca 1120. Mathilde died on 2 Jan 1145; she was 25. [6] Occupation: Gräfin.

Friedrich Barbarossa Von Schwaben

3141540 Friedrich Barbarossa Von Schwaben. [1] Born in 1122. Friedrich Barbarossa died on 10 Jun 1190; he was 68. Occupation: Kaiser.

Friedrich participated in the third crusade.

Friedrich Barbarossa married **Beatrix Von Burgund** [1].

They had the following children:
1570770   i.   Philipp (ca1178-1208)
            ii.   Beatrix [6] (ca1160-<1174)
           iii.   Friedrich [6] (ca1164-ca1168)

iv.	Heinrich IV. [6] (1165-1197)	
v.	Otto I. [6] (1170-1200)	
vi.	Konrad [6] (1172-1196)	
vii.	Rainald [6]	
viii.	Wilhelm [6]	
ix.	Agnes [6] (ca1178-1184)	

Beatrix Von Burgund

3141541 Beatrix Von Burgund. [1] Born in 1145. Beatrix died on 15 Nov 1184; she was 39.

23rd Generation

---❖---

5456560 Walram III. Paganus von Limburg. [3] Born in 1099. Walram III. Paganus died on 16 Jul 1139; he was 40. Occupation: Graf, Herzog von Niederlothringen.

Walram III. Paganus married **Jutta von Geldern** [3].

They had the following children:

2728280	i.	Heinrich II. (ca1110-1167)
	ii.	Gerhard I. [6]
	iii.	Beatrix [6] (->1164)
	iv.	Walram IV. [6] (->1145)

5456561 Jutta von Geldern. [3] Occupation: Gräfin.

Friedrich II. Der Einäugige Von Hohenstaufen

6283080 Friedrich II. Der Einäugige Von Hohenstaufen. [1] Born in 1090. Friedrich II. Der Einäugige died in 1147; he was 57. Occupation: Herzog von Schwaben.

In 1120 when Friedrich II. Der Einäugige was 30, he married **Judith Von Bayern** [1].

They had the following children:
3141540   i.   Friedrich Barbarossa (1122-1190)
           ii.   Bertha [6] (-ca1194)

6283081 Judith Von Bayern. [1] Judith died ca 1130.

24th Generation
— ❖ —

10913120 Heinrich I. von Limburg. [3] Born in 1082. Heinrich I. died in 1119; he was 37. Occupation: Graf, Pfalzgraf am Rhein.

Heinrich I. married **Adelheid von Pottenstein** [3].

They had the following children:
5456560   i.   Walram III. Paganus (1099-1139)
           ii.   Agnes [6] (-1136)
           iii.   Adelheid [6] (-ca1145)
           iv.   Mathilde [6]

10913121 Adelheid von Pottenstein. [3] Occupation: Gräfin, aus dem Hause der Sachsenkeiser.

12566160 Friedrich I. Von Hohenstaufen. [1] Born in 1050. Friedrich I. died in 1105; he was 55. Occupation: Herzog von Schwaben.

In 1086 when Friedrich I. was 36, he married **Agnes Von Waiblingen** [1].

They had the following children:

6283080	i.	Friedrich II. Der Einäugige (1090-1147)
	ii.	Heilika [6] (->1110)
	iii.	Bertrada [6] (ca1088-<1142)
	iv.	Hildegardis [6]
	v.	Konrad III. [6] (1093-1152)
	vi.	Gisela [6]
	vii.	Heinrich [6] (-<1102)
	viii.	Beatrix [6]
	ix.	Kunigunde [6]
	x.	Sophia [6]
	xi.	Gertrud [6]

Agnes Von Waiblingen

12566161 Agnes Von Waiblingen. [1] Born ca 1072. Agnes died on 24 Sep 1143; she was 71. Occupation: Herzogin von Schwaben und Markgräfin von Österreich.

25th Generation

21826240 Walram II. von Limburg. [3] Born ca 1061. Walram II. died in 1070; he was 9. Occupation: Graf von Limburg.

Walram II. married **Jutta von Luxemburg** [3].

They had the following children:

10913120   i.   Heinrich I. (1082-1119)

              ii.   Konrad [6]

21826241 Jutta von Luxemburg. [3] Occupation: Gräfin.

Heinrich IV. Von Waiblingen

25132322 Heinrich IV. Von Waiblingen. [1] Born on 11 Nov 1050. Heinrich IV. died on 7 Aug 1106; he was 55. Occupation: Römisch-Deutscher Kaiser.

On 13 Jul 1066 when Heinrich IV. was 15, he married **Bertha Von Savoyen** [1].

They had the following children:

12566161   i.   Agnes (ca1072-1143)

              ii.   Adelheid [6] (1070-<1079)

              iii.   Heinrich [6] (1071-1071)

              iv.   Konrad III. (1074-1101)

              v.   Heinrich V. (1086-1125)

25132323 Bertha Von Savoyen. [1] Born on 21 Sep 1051. Bertha died in Mainz on 27 Dec 1087; she was 36.

26th Generation

43652482 Friedrich II. von Luxemburg. [3] Born ca 1005. Friedrich II. died on 28 Aug 1065; he was 60. Occupation: Graf, Herzog von Niederlothringen.

Friedrich II. married **Gerberga von Brabant**.

They had one child:

21826241   i.   Jutta

43652483 Gerberga von Brabant. Gerberga died ca 1049. Occupation: Herzogin.

Heinrich III. Salier

50264644 Heinrich III. Salier. [1] Born on 28 Oct 1017. Heinrich III. died on 5 Oct 1056; he was 38. Occupation: Römisch-Deutscher Kaiser.

Heinrich III. married **Agnes Von Poitou** [1].

They had the following children:

25132322	i.	Heinrich IV. (1050-1106)
	ii.	Adelheid [6] (1045-1096)
	iii.	Gisela [6] (1047-1053)
	iv.	Mathilde [6] (1048-1060)
	v.	Konrad [6] (1052-1055)
	vi.	Judith [6] (1054-ca1092)

Agnes Von Poitou

50264645 Agnes Von Poitou. [1] Born ca 1025. Agnes died on 14 Dec 1077; she was 52.

27th Generation
--------------- ✛ ---------------

87304966 Eustach I. Boulogne. [6] Born in 1010. Eustach I. died in 1049; he was 39. Occupation: Graf von Boulogne.

Eustach I. married **Mathilde von Brabant** [6].

They had the following children:

43652483	i.	Gerberga (-ca1049)
	ii.	Eustach II. [6] (-1088)
	iii.	Gottfried [6] (-1095)
	iv.	Graf von Lens [6] (-1054)

87304967 Mathilde von Brabant. [6]

Konrad II. Der Ältere Salier

100529288 Konrad II. Der Ältere Salier. [1] Born ca 990. Konrad II. Der Ältere died on 4 Jun 1039; he was 49. Occupation: Römisch-Deutscher Kaiser.

In 1016 when Konrad II. Der Ältere was 26, he married **Gisela Von Schwaben** [1].

They had one child:

50264644	i.	Heinrich III. (1017-1056)

Gisela Von Schwaben

100529289 Gisela Von Schwaben. [1] Born ca 989. Gisela died on 15 Feb 1043; she was 54. Occupation: Deutsche Königin.

28th Generation

Lambert I. von Brabant

174609934 Lambert I. von Brabant. [3] Lambert I. died in 1015. Occupation: Herzog.

ca 987 Lambert I. married **Gerberga von Niederlothringen und Brabant** [3].

They had the following children:
87304967	i.	Mathilde
	ii.	Reginar [6]
	iii.	Lambert II. [6] (-1054)
	iv.	Heinrich I. der Alte [6] (-1038)

Gerberga von Niederlothringen und Brabant

174609935 Gerberga von Niederlothringen und Brabant. [3] Born ca 975.
Gerberga died aft 1018; she was 43. Occupation: Herzogin.

Heinrich Salier

201058576 Heinrich Salier. [1] Heinrich died ca 990. Occupation: Grafen im
Wormsgau.

Heinrich married **Adelheid Matfriede**.

They had the following children:
100529288   i.   Konrad II. Der Ältere (ca990-1039)
              ii.   Judith [6]

Adelheid Matfriede

201058577 Adelheid Matfriede. Adelheid died ca 1039.

29th Generation

— ⁖ —

349219870 Karl von Niederlothringen Karolinger. Born in 953. Karl von Niederlothringen died in 992; he was 39. Occupation: Herzog.

ca 975 when Karl von Niederlothringen was 22, he married **Agnes von Vermandois und der Champagne** [3].

They had the following children:

174609935	i.	Gerberga (ca975->1018)
	ii.	Otto (ca975-ca1005)
	iii.	Ludwig [6] (<989->993)
	iv.	Karl [6] (989->991)
	v.	Adelheid [6] (->1012)

349219871 Agnes von Vermandois und der Champagne. [3]

Otto Salier

402117152 Otto Salier. [1] Born ca 948. Otto died on 4 Nov 1004; he was 56. Occupation: Herzog von Kärnten.

Otto married **Judith Von Kärnten** [1].

They had the following children:

201058576	i.	Heinrich (-ca990)
	ii.	Bruno [6] (972-999)
	iii.	Konrad [6] (-1011)
	iv.	Wilhelm [6] (-ca1046)

402117153 Judith Von Kärnten. [1] Judith died in 991. Occupation: Herzogin von Kärnten.

30th Generation
—————————— ✣ ——————————

Ludwig IV. der Überseeische Karolinger

698439740 Ludwig IV. der Überseeische Karolinger. [3] Born ca 920. Ludwig IV. der Überseeische died on 10 Sep 954; he was 34. Occupation: König von Frankreich.

ca 939 when Ludwig IV. der Überseeische was 19, he married **Gerberga von Lothringen**.

They had the following children:

349219870	i.	Karl von Niederlothringen (Twin) (953-992)
	ii.	Lothar [6] (941-986)
	iii.	Mathilde [6] (943->981)
	iv.	Karl [6] (943-<953)
	v.	Ludwig [6] (948-<954)
	vi.	Heinrich [6] (Twin) (953-953)

Gerberga von Lothringen

698439741 Gerberga von Lothringen. Born in 913. Gerberga died on 5 May 969; she was 56. Occupation: Herzogin von Lothringen und Königin von Frankreich.

804234304 Konrad der Rote Salier. Born ca 922. Konrad der Rote died on 10 Aug 955; he was 33. Occupation: Herzog in Lothringen, Graf in Franken.

In 947 when Konrad der Rote was 25, he married **Liutgard Von Sachsen** [1].

They had one child:
402117152   i.   Otto (ca948-1004)

804234305 Liutgard Von Sachsen. [1] Born in 931. Liutgard died in 953; she was 22.

31st Generation
------------------- ❖ -------------------

Karls III. der Einfältige Karolinger

1396879480 Karls III. der Einfältige Karolinger. Born on 17 Sep 879. Karls III. der Einfältige died in Péronne on 7 Oct 929; he was 50. Occupation: König der Westfranken und von Frankreich.

Karls III. der Einfältige married **Edgifa von Wessex** [3].

They had one child:
698439740   i.   Ludwig IV. der Überseeische (ca920-954)

Edgifa von Wessex

1396879481 Edgifa von Wessex. [3] Born in 903. Edgifa died aft 951; she was 48.

Otto I. Der Grosse Von Sachsen

1608468610 Otto I. Der Grosse Von Sachsen. [1] Born on 23 Nov 912. Otto I. Der Grosse died on 7 May 973; he was 60. Occupation: Römisch-Deutscher Kaiser.

Otto I. Der Grosse married **Edgitha**.

They had the following children:
804234305   i.   Liutgard (931-953)
            ii.   Liudolf [6] (930-957)

Edgitha

1608468611 Edgitha. Born in 910. Edgitha died on 26 Jan 946; she was 36. Occupation: Königin des Ostfrankenreiches.

32nd Generation
———————— ❖ ————————

Ludwig II. der Stammler Karolinger

2793758960 Ludwig II. der Stammler Karolinger. [3] Born on 1 Nov 846. Ludwig II. der Stammler died on 10 Apr 879; he was 32. Occupation: König von Frankreich.

Ludwig II. der Stammler married **Adelheid Adalharde** [3].

They had the following children:
1396879480   i.   Karls III. der Einfältige (879-929)
              ii.   Ermentrud [6] (ca875-)

2793758961 Adelheid Adalharde. [3]

Heinrich I. Liudolfinger

3216937220 Heinrich I. Liudolfinger. [1] Born in 876. Heinrich I. died on 2 Jul 936; he was 60. Occupation: König des Ostfrankenreiches.

Heinrich I. married **Mathilde Die Heilige Immedinger** [1].

They had the following children:

1608468610	i.	Otto I. Der Grosse (912-973)
	ii.	Brun [6] (925-965)
	iii.	Gerberga [6] (913-969)
	iv.	Hadwig [6] (ca914-959)

Mathilde Die Heilige Immedinger

3216937221 Mathilde Die Heilige Immedinger. [1] Born ca 895. Mathilde Die Heilige died on 14 Mar 968; she was 73.

33rd Generation

Karl II. der Kahle Karolinger

5587517920 Karl II. der Kahle Karolinger. [3] Born on 13 Jun 823 in Frankfurt am Main. Karl II. der Kahle died on 6 Oct 877; he was 54. Occupation:

Westfränkischer König (843-877) und König von Italien und römischer Kaiser (875-877).

On 14 Dec 842 when Karl II. der Kahle was 19, he married **Irmentrud von Orléans** [3]. They were divorced in 867.

They had the following children:

2793758960	i.	Ludwig II. der Stammler (846-879)
	ii.	Judith [6] (ca844->870)
	iii.	Karl das Kind [6] (ca849-866)
	iv.	Karlmann (-876)
	v.	Lothar [6] (-865)
	vi.	Ermentrud [6] (->877)
	vii.	Hildegard [6]
	viii.	Gisela [6]
	ix.	Rotrud [6]

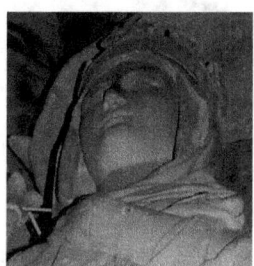

Irmentrud von Orléans

5587517921 Irmentrud von Orléans. [3] Born on 27 Sep 825. Irmentrud died on 6 Oct 869; she was 44.

Otto I. Der Erlauchte Liudolfinger

6433874440 Otto I. Der Erlauchte Liudolfinger. [1] Born bef 866. Otto I. Der Erlauchte died on 30 Nov 912; he was 46. Occupation: Herzog von Sachsen.

Otto I. Der Erlauchte married **Hadwig Babenberger** [1].

They had the following children:

3216937220	i.	Heinrich I. (876-936)
	ii.	Oda
	iii.	Thankmar [6] (-<912)
	iv.	Liudolf [6] (-<912)

6433874441 Hadwig Babenberger. [1] Hadwig died on 24 Dec 903.

34th Generation

Ludwig I. der Fromme Karolinger

11175035840 Ludwig I. der Fromme Karolinger. Born in 778. Ludwig I. der Fromme died on 20 Jun 840; he was 62. Occupation: Römischer Kaiser (813–840).

Ludwig I. der Fromme married **Judith von Bayern** [3].

They had the following children:

| 5587517920 | i. | Karl II. der Kahle (823-877) |
| | ii. | Gisela [6] (820-874) |

95

Judith von Bayern

11175035841 Judith von Bayern. [3] Born in 795. Judith died in 843; she was 48.

Liudolf Liudolfinger

12867748880 Liudolf Liudolfinger. [8] Born ca 805. Liudolf died on 12 Mar 866; he was 61. Occupation: Graf in Sachsen.

Liudolf married **Oda Billunger** [6].

They had the following children:

6433874440	i.	Otto I. Der Erlauchte (<866-912)
	ii.	Liutgard [8] (-855)
	iii.	Brun [6]
	iv.	Thankmar [6]
	v.	Liutgard [6] (-885)
	vi.	Hathumod [6] (840-874)
	vii.	Gerberga [6] (-896)
	viii.	Christina [6] (-919)

12867748881 Oda Billunger. [6]

35th Generation

Karl der Grosse Karolinger

22350071680 Karl der Grosse Karolinger. [3] Born ca 747. Karl der Grosse died on 28 Jan 814; he was 67. Occupation: Römischer Kaiser.

Karl der Grosse married **Hildegard von Anglachgau** [3].

They had the following children:

11175035840	i.	Ludwig I. der Fromme (778-840)
	ii.	Karl der Jüngere [6] (ca772-811)
	iii.	Adalhaid [6] (ca773-ca774)
	iv.	Rotrud [6] (ca775-810)
	v.	Karlmann [6] (777-810)
	vi.	Lothar [6] (ca778-ca779)
	vii.	Bertha [6] (775->828)
	viii.	Gisela [6] (781->800)
	ix.	Hildegard [6] (782-783)

Hildegard von Anglachgau

22350071681 Hildegard von Anglachgau. [3] Born in 758. Hildegard died on 30 Apr 783; she was 25.

36th Generation

Pippin der Kleine Karolinger

44700143360 Pippin der Kleine Karolinger. [3] Born in 714. Pippin der Kleine died on 24 Sep 768; he was 54. Occupation: König der Franken.

Pippin der Kleine married **Bertrada die Jüngere von Laon** [3].

They had the following children:

22350071680	i.	Karl der Grosse (ca747-814)
	ii.	Karlmann I. [6] (751-771)
	iii.	Gisela [6] (757-810)
	iv.	Pippin [6] (759-761)
	v.	Rothaid [6]
	vi.	Adelheid [6]

Bertrada die Jüngere von Laon

44700143361 Bertrada die Jüngere von Laon. [3] Bertrada die Jüngere died in 783.

37th Generation

Karl Martell Karolinger

89400286720 Karl Martell Karolinger. [3] Born ca 686. Karl Martell died on 22 Oct 741; he was 55. Occupation: König von Frankreich.

Karl Martell married **Rotrude von Trier** [3].

They had the following children:
44700143360	i.	Pippin der Kleine (714-768)
	ii.	Karlmann [6] (-754)
	iii.	Hiltrud [6] (715-754)

89400286721 Rotrude von Trier. [3] Born in 690. Rotrude died in 724; she was 34.

38th Generation

Pippin von Herstal Arnulfinger

178800573440 Pippin von Herstal Arnulfinger. [3] Born ca 635. Pippin von Herstal died on 14 Dec 714; he was 79. Occupation: König der Franken.

Pippin von Herstal married **Alpais** [3].

They had one child:
89400286720 i. Karl Martell (ca686-741)

178800573441 Alpais. [3]

39th Generation
——————— ❖ ———————

357601146880 Ansegisel Arnulfinger. [3] Born ca 610. Ansegisel died ca 662; he was 52.

Ansegisel married **Begga die Heilige von Heristal** [3].

They had one child:
178800573440 i. Pippin von Herstal (ca635-714)

Begga die Heilige von Heristal

357601146881 Begga die Heilige von Heristal. [3] Born ca 620. Begga die Heilige died ca 693; she was 73.

40th Generation
——————— ❖ ———————

Arnulf von Metz Arnulfinger

715202293760 Arnulf von Metz Arnulfinger. [3] Born ca 584. Arnulf von Metz died ca 641; he was 57. Occupation: Bischof von Metz.

Children:
357601146880   i.   Ansegisel (ca610-ca662)
             ii.   Chlodulf [6] (-ca656)

Sources

1. Dr. Wilhelm Thöne, "Geschichte Der Familie Thöne," 3, 1938.
2. Kirchenbuch Paderborn Wewer, St. Johannes Baptist, Diözesanarchiv Paderborn.
3. "Die Ahnenreihe der Familie Meiwes," Dr. Wilhelm Thöne.
4. Leopold von Ledebur, Diplomatische Geschichte der Stadt und Herrschaft Vlotho, Raud's Buchhandlung, 1829.
5. Detlev Schwennicke, Europäische Stammtafeln XXVIII, Vittorio Klostermann.
6. Everyone, "Wikipedia," http://www.wikipedia.org.
7. "Familienbuch Bartneck Rother."
8. Andreas Hansert, Könige und Kaiser in Deutschland und Österreich, Imhof, 2006.

Index

Hildegard (von) (758 - 783)   22350071681

Arnulfinger

Ansegisel (ca610 - ca662)   357601146880
Arnulf von Metz (ca584 - ca641)   715202293760
Pippin von Herstal (ca635 - 714)   178800573440

Babenberger

Hadwig (- 903)   6433874441

Bayern

Judith (Von) (- ca1130)   6283081
Judith (von) (795 - 843)   11175035841

Bernsau zum Hardeberg

Margarete (Von)   191
Wilhelm (Von) (- 1572)   382

Billunger

Oda   12867748881

Bose

Everhard Wilhelm (Von) (1655 - 1710)   10
Franz Dietrich (Von) (1690 -)   20
George (Von)   40
Katharina Maria (Von) (1705 - 1758)   5

Boulogne

Eustach I. (1010 - 1049)   87304966
Eustach II. (- 1088)   child of 87304966
Gottfried (- 1095)   child of 87304966
Graf von Lens (- 1054)   child of 87304966

Brabant

Alix (Von) (- 1315)   child of 196346
Beatrix (Von) (1225 - 1288)   child of 785384
Blanche (Von) (- 1329)   child of 196346
Elisabeth (Von) (1303 - <1350)   98173
Gerberga (von) (- ca1049)   43652483
Gottfried (Von) (ca1267 - 1302)   196346
Heinrich I. der Alte (von) (- 1038)   child of 174609934
Heinrich II. der Grossmütige (Von) (1207 - 1248)   785384
Heinrich III. Der Friedfertige (Von) (ca1231 - 1261)   392692
Heinrich IV. (Von) (1251 - 1272)   child of 392692
Johan I. der Siegreiche (Von) (1253 - 1294)   child of 392692
Johann (Von) (1281 - 1302)   child of 196346
Johanna (Von) (- >1318)   child of 196346
Lambert I. (von) (- 1015)   174609934

Lambert II. (von) (- 1054)	child of 174609934
Margarete (Von) (- >1318)	child of 196346
Margarethe (Von) (- 1277)	child of 785384
Maria (Von) (- 1330)	child of 196346
Maria (Von) (ca1226 - 1256)	child of 785384
Maria (Von) (1256 - 1321)	child of 392692
Mathilde (von)	87304967
Mathilde (Von) (1224 - 1288)	child of 785384
Philip (Von)	child of 785384
Reginar (von)	child of 174609934

Büren

Bernhard (von) (- 1551)	1332
Bernhard (von) (1443 - 1478)	5328
Johann (von) (- 1481)	2664
Theodora (von)	333

Büren-Davensberg

Wilhelm (von)	10656

Burgund

Adelheid (Von) (1233 - 1273)	392693
Beatrix (Von) (1145 - 1184)	3141541
Hugo IV (Von)	785386

Byzanz

Irene Marie (Von) (ca1177 - 1208)	1570771

Claes

Anna Maria Elisabeth (1751 - 1814)	3

Dormund

Kunigunde (von)	85259

Drewes

Anton Bernhard (1720 - 1763)	4
Franz Anton (1751 - 1789)	2
Maria Anna Juliana Antonette (1780 - 1846)	1

Edelherr von Büren

Johann (- 1592)	666

Efferen

Sybilla (Von)	95

Efferen zu Disternich

Adolf (Von) (1549 - <1582)	190

Ense

Eva Dorothea (von)	83

Heinrich (von) (- 1592)	332

Westkotten
Walther Philipp (von) (1628 -)	166

Geldern
Jutta (von)	5456561

Gemen
Johann (Von) (1405 - 1455)	6134
Katharina (Von) (1442 - 1496)	3067

Gudenberg
N. Wolf (von) (- 1484)	2665

Helling
Caspar Cornelius (- 1695)	22
Maria	11

Heristal
Begga die Heilige (von) (ca620 - ca693)	357601146881

Hohenstaufen
Beatrix (Von)	child of 12566160
Bertha (Von) (- ca1194)	child of 6283080
Bertrada (Von) (ca1088 - <1142)	child of 12566160
Friedrich I. (Von) (1050 - 1105)	12566160
Friedrich II. Der Einäugige (Von) (1090 - 1147)	6283080
Gertrud (Von)	child of 12566160
Gisela (Von)	child of 12566160
Heilika (Von) (- >1110)	child of 12566160
Heinrich (Von) (- <1102)	child of 12566160
Hildegardis (Von)	child of 12566160
Konrad III. (Von) (1093 - 1152)	child of 12566160
Kunigunde (Von)	child of 12566160
Maria (Von) (- 1235)	785385
Sophia (Von)	child of 12566160

Holland
Johanna (Von) (1315 - 1374)	49087

Hörde zu Schwarzengraben
Mathilde (von)	667

Hörde zu Störmede und Ehringerfeld
Katharina (von)	167

Horn
Oda (Von)	6135
Wilhelm (Von) (1377 - 1455)	12270

Horst

Arnold (Von Der) (- 1641)	46
Hedewig (Von Der) (- <1693)	23

Immedinger

Mathilde Die Heilige (ca895 - 968)	3216937221

Isenburg

Agnes (von)	child of 341034
Dietrich (von) (ca1215 - 1301)	child of 341034
Elisabeth (von)	child of 341034
Friedrich (von)	child of 341034
Friedrich (von) (<1193 - 1226)	341034
Sophie (von)	170517

Jülich

Elisabeth (Von)	child of 98172
Gerhard V. (Von) (1279 - 1328)	98172
Gerhard VI. (Von) (- 1360)	child of 49086
Gottfried (Von) (- 1335)	child of 98172
Heinrich (Von) (1319 - 1334)	child of 98172
Isabella (Von) (- 1411)	child of 49086
Johanna (Von) (- <1367)	child of 49086
Marie (Von) (- 1353)	child of 98172
Philippa (Von) (- <1350)	24543
Richardis (Von) (- <1355)	child of 98172
Richardis (Von)	child of 49086
Walram (Von) (1322 - 1349)	child of 98172
Wilhelm II. (Von) (ca1325 - 1393)	child of 49086
Wilhelm V. (Von) (ca1317 - 1361)	49086

Kärnten

Judith (Von) (- 991)	402117153

Karolinger

Adalhaid (ca773 - ca774)	child of 22350071680
Adelheid	child of 44700143360
Adelheid (- >1012)	child of 349219870
Bertha (775 - >828)	child of 22350071680
Ermentrud (- >877)	child of 5587517920
Ermentrud (ca875 -)	child of 2793758960
Gisela	child of 5587517920
Gisela (757 - 810)	child of 44700143360
Gisela (781 - >800)	child of 22350071680
Gisela (820 - 874)	child of 11175035840

Heinrich (953 - 953)	child of 698439740
Hildegard	child of 5587517920
Hildegard (782 - 783)	child of 22350071680
Hiltrud (715 - 754)	child of 89400286720
Judith (ca844 - >870)	child of 5587517920
Karl (943 - <953)	child of 698439740
Karl (989 - >991)	child of 349219870
Karl das Kind (ca849 - 866)	child of 5587517920
Karl der Grosse (ca747 - 814)	22350071680
Karl der Jüngere (ca772 - 811)	child of 22350071680
Karl II. der Kahle (823 - 877)	5587517920
Karl Martell (ca686 - 741)	89400286720
Karl von Niederlothringen (953 - 992)	349219870
Karlmann (- 754)	child of 89400286720
Karlmann (- 876)	child of 5587517920
Karlmann (777 - 810)	child of 22350071680
Karlmann I. (751 - 771)	child of 44700143360
Karls III. der Einfältige (879 - 929)	1396879480
Lothar (- 865)	child of 5587517920
Lothar (ca778 - ca779)	child of 22350071680
Lothar (941 - 986)	child of 698439740
Ludwig (948 - <954)	child of 698439740
Ludwig (<989 - >993)	child of 349219870
Ludwig I. der Fromme (778 - 840)	11175035840
Ludwig II. der Stammler (846 - 879)	2793758960
Ludwig IV. der Überseeische (ca920 - 954)	698439740
Mathilde (943 - >981)	child of 698439740
Otto (ca975 - ca1005)	child of 349219870
Pippin (759 - 761)	child of 44700143360
Pippin der Kleine (714 - 768)	44700143360
Rothaid	child of 44700143360
Rotrud	child of 5587517920
Rotrud (ca775 - 810)	child of 22350071680

Laon

Bertrada die Jüngere (von) (- 783)	44700143361

Limburg

Adelheid (von) (- ca1145)	child of 10913120
Agnes (von) (- 1136)	child of 10913120
Beatrix (von) (- >1164)	child of 5456560
Friederich (von)	child of 1364140
Gerhard I. (von)	child of 5456560
Gerhard II. (von) (- 1225)	child of 1364140

Heinrich I. (von) (1082 - 1119)	10913120
Heinrich II. (von) (ca1110 - 1167)	2728280
Heinrich III. (von) (ca1140 - 1221)	1364140
Heinrich IV. (von) (- 1247)	child of 682070
Heinrich IV. (von) (ca1165 - 1214)	child of 1364140
Isabella (von) (- 1221)	child of 1364140
Judith (von) (- 1202)	child of 1364140
Konrad (von)	child of 21826240
Macharius (von)	child of 1364140
Mathilde (von)	child of 10913120
Mathilde (von)	child of 682070
Simon (von) (1178 - 1195)	child of 1364140
Sophie (von) (- 1226)	341035
Walram II. (von) (ca1061 - 1070)	21826240
Walram III. Paganus (von) (1099 - 1139)	5456560
Walram IV. (von) (- >1145)	child of 5456560
Walram IV. (von) (1198 - 1226)	682070

Liudolfinger

Brun	child of 12867748880
Brun (925 - 965)	child of 3216937220
Christina (- 919)	child of 12867748880
Gerberga (- 896)	child of 12867748880
Gerberga (913 - 969)	child of 3216937220
Hadwig (ca914 - 959)	child of 3216937220
Hathumod (840 - 874)	child of 12867748880
Heinrich I. (876 - 936)	3216937220
Liudolf (- <912)	child of 6433874440
Liudolf (ca805 - 866)	12867748880
Liutgard (- 855)	child of 12867748880
Liutgard (- 885)	child of 12867748880
Oda	child of 6433874440
Otto I. Der Erlauchte (<866 - 912)	6433874440
Thankmar	child of 12867748880
Thankmar (- <912)	child of 6433874440

Loos

Dorothea (Von)	12271
Gottfried Graf (Von) (1357 - 1395)	24542

Lothringen

Gerberga (von) (913 - 969)	698439741
Sophie (von) (ca1149 - >1215)	1364141

Luxemburg

Friedrich II. (von) (ca1005 - 1065)	43652482
Jutta (von)	21826241

Matfriede

Adelheid (- ca1039)	201058577

Merode zu Bornheim

Barbera Scheiffart (Von)	767

Metz

Chlodulf (von) (- ca656)	child of 715202293760

Monschau

Kunigunde (von)	682071
Walram II. (von) (- 1242)	child of 682070

Nesselrode-Stein

Irmgrad (von)	1533
Johann (von) (1442 - 1498)	3066

Niederlothringen und Brabant

Gerberga (von) (ca975 - >1018)	174609935

Orléans

Irmentrud (von) (825 - 869)	5587517921

Plettenberg zu Schönrad

Anna (Von)	383
Bertold (Von) (1444 - 1477)	1532
Dietrich (Von) (- 1521)	766

Poitou

Agnes (Von) (ca1025 - 1077)	50264645

Pottenstein

Adelheid (von)	10913121

Rüspe

Anna Margareta (Von) (- >1641)	47

Rüspe zu Brüninghausen

Christoph (Von) (- 1614)	94

Sachsen

Liudolf (Von) (930 - 957)	child of 1608468610
Liutgard (Von) (931 - 953)	804234305
Otto I. Der Grosse (Von) (912 - 973)	1608468610

Saffenberg

Mathilde (von) (ca1120 - 1145)	2728281

Salier

Adelheid (1045 - 1096)	child of 50264644

Bruno (972 - 999)	child of 402117152
Gisela (1047 - 1053)	child of 50264644
Heinrich (- ca990)	201058576
Heinrich III. (1017 - 1056)	50264644
Judith	child of 201058576
Judith (1054 - ca1092)	child of 50264644
Konrad (- 1011)	child of 402117152
Konrad (1052 - 1055)	child of 50264644
Konrad der Rote (ca922 - 955)	804234304
Konrad II. Der Ältere (ca990 - 1039)	100529288
Mathilde (1048 - 1060)	child of 50264644
Otto (ca948 - 1004)	402117152
Wilhelm (- ca1046)	child of 402117152

Savoyen
Bertha (Von) (1051 - 1087)	25132323

Sayn
Gottfried (von) (1324 - 1354)	42628

Sayn-Wittgenstein
Margaretha (von)	10657
Salentin (von) (1340 - 1386)	21314

Schwaben
Agnes (Von) (ca1178 - 1184)	child of 3141540
Beatrix (Von) (ca1160 - <1174)	child of 3141540
Beatrix (Von) (1198 - 1212)	child of 1570770
Beatrix Posthuma (Von) (1208 -)	child of 1570770
Elisabeth (Von) (1203 - 1235)	child of 1570770
Friedrich (Von) (ca1164 - ca1168)	child of 3141540
Friedrich (Von) (1206 -)	child of 1570770
Friedrich Barbarossa (Von) (1122 - 1190)	3141540
Gisela (Von) (ca989 - 1043)	100529289
Heinrich IV. (Von) (1165 - 1197)	child of 3141540
Konrad (Von) (1172 - 1196)	child of 3141540
Kunigunde (Von) (1200 - 1248)	child of 1570770
Otto I. (Von) (1170 - 1200)	child of 3141540
Philipp (Von) (ca1178 - 1208)	1570770
Rainald (Von)	child of 3141540
Rainald (Von)	child of 1570770
Wilhelm (Von)	child of 3141540

Thöne
Anna Maria Theresia (1808 - 1841)	child of 1
Anna Maria Theresia (1813 - 1867)	child of 1

Bernhard Gen. Mühlenburs (1810 - 1885)   child of 1
Johann Ferdinand gen. Stellbrink (1766 - 1813)   spouse of 1
Johannes Christophorus gen. Stellbrink (1803 - 1882)   child of 1
Maria Elisabeth (1805 -)   child of 1

Trier
Rotrude (von) (690 - 724)   89400286721

Vermandois und der Champagne
Agnes (von)   349219871

Vierson und Mesiers
Johanna (Von)   196347

Volmarstein
Dietrich I. (von) (1250 - 1314)   85258
Heinrich III (von) (1209 - 1250)   170516

Vomarstein
Sophie (von)   42629

Waiblingen
Adelheid (Von) (1070 - <1079)   child of 25132322
Agnes (Von) (ca1072 - 1143)   12566161
Heinrich (Von) (1071 - 1071)   child of 25132322
Heinrich IV. (Von) (1050 - 1106)   25132322
Heinrich V. (Von) (1086 - 1125)   child of 25132322
Konrad III. (Von) (1074 - 1101)   child of 25132322

Wesphalen zu Fürstenberg
Willa (von) (1426 -)   5329

Wesphalen zu Herbram
Bernhard (von) (1648 - 1682)   82
Elisabeth Margarethe (von)   41

Wessex
Edgifa (von) (903 - >951)   1396879481

Wigand
Sibilla   21

Wittgenstein
Adelheid (von)   21315

Wrede zu Mylinghausen
Alfradis (von)   1333

The Bartneck Ancestors

First Generation

—————— ✢ ——————

1 K. D. Bartneck (Living, Male).

Second Generation

—————— ✢ ——————

Paul Wilhelm Bartneck

2 Paul Wilhelm Bartneck. Born on 25 Nov 1909 in Großburg, Strehlen, Schlesien. Standesamt Grafsburg Nr. 45/1909. Paul Wilhelm died in Paderborn on 7 Jul 1980; he was 70. Occupation: Oberfeldwebel. [1]

The Bundesarchive has no NSDAP record of Paul Wilhelm Bartneck.

Military: Paul served in the German Army in the 5. Kompanie Panzer-Regiment 11. He operated in the Netherlands, Belgium, Germany and White Russia. He was wounded on December 14th, 1942 with a shrapnel at his head. He was returned back to Paderborn and continued to serve in the army. In 1943 he was returned into the active troops (Panzer Abteilung 505). He then served in Russia, Ukraine, Normandie and Germany. He was registered by a British Release unit, but no details of any war imprisonment is available.

On 28 May 1938 when Paul Wilhelm was 28, he married **Amalie Frieda Rother** in Strehlen, Strehlen, Schlesien. [2] Standesamt Strehlen Nr. 26/1938.

They had the following children:

	i.	Hannelore Auguste (1939-2004)
	ii.	D. U. (Living, Female)
1	iii.	K. D. (Living, Male)
	iv.	Paul Norbert (1945-1945)

Amalie Frieda Rother

3 Amalie Frieda Rother. Amalie Frieda died in Paderborn on 26 Sep 1981; she was 68. Born on 17 Oct 1912 in Waldneudorf, Strehlen, Schlesien. [3] Standesamt Schönjohnsdorf Nr. 44/1912.

Third Generation

4 August Bartneck. [6]

August married **Anna Gnädig** [6].

They had one child:

2	i.	Paul Wilhelm (1909-1980)

5 Anna Gnädig. [6]

Robert Martin Engelberg Rother

6 Robert Martin Engelberg Rother. Robert Martin Engelberg died in Paderborn on 15 May 1956; he was 81. [5] Born on 7 Nov 1874 in Bielefeld-Jöllenbeck, Bielefeld. [5] Standesamt Breslau II Nr. 440.

On 4 Sep 1900 when Robert Martin Engelberg was 25, he married **Anna Martha Auguste Lache** in Breslau, Breslau, Schlesien. [5] Standesamt Breslau II Nr. 570.

They had the following children:

3	i.	Amalie Frieda (1912-1981)
	ii.	Fritz Engelbert (1903-1995)
	iii.	Amalie (1902-1991)

Anna Martha Auguste Lache

7 Anna Martha Auguste Lache. Born on 6 Jun 1878 in Breslau, Breslau, Schlesien. [5] Standesamt Breslau I Nr. 461. Anna Martha Auguste died on 13 Feb 1943; she was 64. [5]

Fourth Generation
———— ❖ ————

12 Johan Gotlob Robert Rother. Born on 26 Jun 1848. [5]

Johan Gotlob Robert married **Anna Louisa Carolina Lache**.

They had the following children:

6	i.	Robert Martin Engelberg (1874-1956)
	ii.	Fritz
	iii.	Otto

13 Anna Louisa Carolina Lache. Born on 9 Mar 1851. [5]

14 Johan Karl Heinrich Lache. Born on 21 Feb 1852. [5] Occupation: Fabrikarbeiter.

On 5 Jun 1876 when Johan Karl Heinrich was 24, he married **Josefine Deutscher**. [5]

They had one child:

| 7 | i. | Anna Martha Auguste (1878-1943) |

15 Josefine Deutscher. Born on 23 Mar 1856 in Krietern. [5]

Fifth Generation

24 Johan Gotlob Rother.

On 8 Oct 1848 Johan Gotlob married **Anna Rosina Bosen**. [5]

They had one child:

| 12 | i. | Johan Gotlob Robert (1848-) |

25 Anna Rosina Bosen. Born on 31 Jul 1822 in Schliesa, Breslau, Schlesien. [5]

26 Gottlieb Lache.

Gottlieb married **Louisa Carolina Schütte**.

They had one child:

| 13 | i. | Anna Louisa Carolina (1851-) |

27 Louisa Carolina Schütte.

Sixth Generation

————————— ✜ —————————

50 Gotlieb Bosen.

Gotlieb married **Elenora Hilbig**.

They had one child:

25	i.	Anna Rosina (1822-)

51 Elenora Hilbig.

Sources

1. "Deutsche Dienststelle," Jan 18, 2011.
2. "Familienbuch Bartneck Rother."
3. "Familienbuch Rother."
4. <u>Kirchenbuch Grossburg</u>, Evangelisches Zentralarchive Berlin.

Index

Rother

Schütte

The Masuoka Ancestors

First Generation

— ❖ —

1 M. 真. Masuoka 益岡 (Living, Female).

Second Generation

— ❖ —

2 T. 達. Masuoka 益岡 (Living, Male).

3 E. 江. Hosokawa 細川 (Living, Female).

Third Generation

— ❖ —

Yasutaka 康隆 Masuoka 益岡

4 Yasutaka 康隆 Masuoka 益岡. Born on 8 Jul 1918 in Chofu, Shimonoseki city, Yamaguchi. Yasutaka 康隆 died in Yono city, Saitama, on 7 May 2003; he was 84.

On 28 May 1945 when Yasutaka 康隆 was 26, he married **Kazue 一枝 Kawakata 河方** in Chofu Shimonoseki-city Yamaguchi.

They had the following children:

- 2   i.   T. 達. (Living, Male)
-    ii.   Y. 康. (Living, Female)
-    iii.   H. 裕. (Living, Male)
-    iv.   T. 徹. (Living, Male)
-    v.   M. み. (Living, Female)

Kazue 一枝 Kawakata 河方

5 Kazue 一枝 Kawakata 河方. Born on 1 Jan 1921 in Taipei city, Taiwan. Kazue 一枝 died in Tsuwano town, Shimane,Japan, on 22 May 2009; she was 88.

Shigenori 重憲 Hosokawa 細川

6 Shigenori 重憲 Hosokawa 細川. Born on 4 May 1921 in Takayacho,Kannonnji city,Kagawa. Shigenori 重憲 died in Hikaridai, Seika cho,Kyoto, on 26 Nov 2006; he was 85.

On 25 Nov 1947 when Shigenori 重憲 was 26, he married **K. キ. Iwata 岩田 (Living, Female)**.

They had the following children:

3	i.	E. 江. (Living, Female)
	ii.	K. 和. (Living, Female)
	iii.	H. 英. (Living, Male)
	iv.	H. 英. (Living, Male)

7 K. キ. Iwata 岩田 (Living, Female).

Fourth Generation

Waichi 和一 Masuoka 益岡

8 Waichi 和一 Masuoka 益岡. Born on 22 Jan 1893 in Chofu, Shimonoseki city, Yamaguchi.

Waichi 和一 married **Machi マチ Nakamura 中村**.

They had one child:

4	i.	Yasutaka 康隆 (1918-2003)

9 Machi マチ Nakamura 中村. Machi マチ died on 8 Oct 1920.

10 Nobuo 述雄 Kawakata 河方.

Nobuo 述雄 married **Chizu チヅ Etoh 衛藤**.

They had the following children:

    5   i.   Kazue 一枝 (1921-2009)

           ii.   Yasuo 泰雄

11 Chizu チヅ Etoh 衛藤.

Tsunehiko 常彦 Hosokawa 細川

12 Tsunehiko 常彦 Hosokawa 細川. Born on 17 Oct 1877.

Tsunehiko 常彦 married **Teru テル- Iwata 岩田**.

They had the following children:

    6   i.   Shigenori 重憲 (1921-2006)

           ii.   Toshiaki 利明 (1910-)

           iii.   Takehisa 竹久 (1919-)

           iv.   Isano イサノ (1902-)

           v.   Shizue シズエ (1903-)

           vi.   Sadae サダエ (1905-)

           vii.   Sueno スエノ (1914-)

Teru テル- Iwata 岩田

13 Teru テル- Iwata 岩田. Born on 8 May 1883.

Teru is the biolagical mother of Tsunehiko's children, although she is not registered as his official wife.

Fukujiro 福二郎 Iwata 岩田

14 Fukujiro 福二郎 Iwata 岩田.

Fukujiro 福二郎 married **Suga スガ Kubo 久保**.

They had the following children:

7	i.	Kiyoe キヨエ (1925-)
	ii.	Teijirou 禎二郎
	iii.	Yorie よりえ
	iv.	Bunichi 文市
	v.	Kouzou 恒造

Suga スガ Kubo 久保

15 Suga スガ Kubo 久保.

Fifth Generation

———————— ✣ ————————

Wakichi 和吉 Masuoka 益岡

16 Wakichi 和吉 Masuoka 益岡. Born in Chofu, Shimonoseki city, Yamaguchi. Wakichi 和吉 died on 28 Apr 1944.

Wakichi 和吉 married **Tatsu タツ**.

They had one child:
      8   i.   Waichi 和一 (1893-)

17 Tatsu タツ.

20 Somon 素門 Kawakata 河方.

Child:
>   **10**   i.   Nobuo 述雄

24 Yahei 弥平 Hosokawa 細川.

Yahei 弥平 married **Shigeno シゲノ**.

They had the following children:
>   **12**   i.   Tsunehiko 常彦 (1877-)
>
>   ii.   Kengo 健吾
>
>   iii.   Rie リエ
>
>   iv.   Kane カネ
>
>   v.   Tami タミ

25 Shigeno シゲノ.

26 Seiji 清治 Iwata 岩田.

Seiji 清治 married **Riki リキ**.

They had the following children:
>   i.   Matsu マツ
>
>   **13**   ii.   Teru テル- (1883-)

27 Riki リキ.

Sixth Generation
❖

32 Toubei 藤兵衛 Masuoka 益岡.

Child:
>   **16**   i.   Wakichi 和吉 (-1944)

40 Juzaemonn 十左衛門 Kawakata 河方.

Child:
    20   i.   Somon 素門

48 Eisuke 栄助 Hosokawa 細川.

Eisuke 栄助 married **Etsu エツ**.

They had one child:
    24   i.   Yahei 弥平

49 Etsu エツ.

Seventh Generation
—————— ✤ ——————

80 Gennbei 源兵衛 Kawakata 河方.

Child:
    40   i.   Juzaemonn 十左衛門

96 Yasuzou 安城 Hosokawa 細川.

Child:
    48   i.   Eisuke 栄助

Eighth Generation
—————— ✤ ——————

160 Bunnki 文喜 Kawakata 河方.

Child:
    80   i.   Gennbei 源兵衛

192 Tsunehachi 常八 Hosokawa 細川.

Child:
    96   i.   Yasuzou 安城

Ninth Generation

320 Asauemonn 浅右衛門 Kawakata 河方.

Child:
    160   i.   Bunnki 文喜

384 Hosokawa 細川.

Children:
    192   i.   Tsunehachi 常八
             ii.   Kyuzaemon 九佐エ門

Tenth Generation

640 Tanshichi 丹七 Kawakata 河方.

Child:
    320   i.   Asauemonn 浅右衛門

Index

Etoh 衛藤

Chizu チヅ   11

Hosokawa 細川

UNNAMED   384
Eisuke 栄助   48

Isano イサノ (1902 -)   child of 12

Kane カネ   child of 24

Kengo 健吾   child of 24

Kyuzaemon 九佐エ門   child of 384

Rie リエ   child of 24

Sadae サダエ (1905 -)   child of 12

Shigenori 重憲 (1921 - 2006)   6

Shizue シズエ (1903 -)   child of 12

Tami タミ   child of 24

Tsunehachi 常八   192

Tsunehiko 常彦 (1877 -)   12

Yahei 弥平   24

Yasuzou 安城   96

Iwata 岩田

Bunichi　文市   child of 14

Fukujiro 福二郎   14

Kouzou 恒造   child of 14

Matsu マツ   child of 26

Seiji 清治   26

Teijirou 禎二郎   child of 14

Teru テル- (1883 -)   13

Yorie　よりえ   child of 14

Kawakata 河方

Asauemonn 浅右衛門   320

Bunnki 文喜   160

Gennbei 源兵衛	80
Juzaemonn 十左衛門	40
Kazue 一枝 (1921 - 2009)	5
Nobuo 述雄	10
Somon 素門	20
Tanshichi 丹七	640
Yasuo 泰雄	child of 10

Kubo 久保

Suga スガ	15

Masuoka 益岡

Toubei 藤兵衛	32
Waichi 和一 (1893 -)	8
Wakichi 和吉 (- 1944)	16
Yasutaka 康隆 (1918 - 2003)	4

Nakamura 中村

Machi マチ (- 1920)	9

Wedding Pictures

Franz Hartman & Theresia Hesse

Wilhelm Bernhard Valentin & Else Link, July 29th, 1919

Eduart Hartman & Maria Klahold

Wilhelm Yacobius Stegemann & Anna Theresia Klahold

Wilhelm Leifeld & Elisabeth Maria

Christian Lorang & Maria Wilhelmina Klahold

Johan Heinrich Hoppe & Johanna Christine Klahold, August 18th, 1943

Heinrich Johannes Klahold & Theresia Menneken

Paul Wilhelm Bartneck & Amalie Frieda Rother, May 28th, 1938

Shigenori Hosokawa & Kiyoe Iwata, November 25th, 1947

www.ingramcontent.com/pod-product-compliance
Lightning Source LLC
Chambersburg PA
CBHW070146290526
45789CB00002B/650